MORE THAN
BREAD AND BUTTER

MORE THAN
BREAD AND BUTTER

A PSYCHOLOGIST SPEAKS TO
PROGRESSIVES ABOUT WHAT PEOPLE
REALLY NEED IN ORDER TO WIN
AND CHANGE THE WORLD

Michael Bader, DMH

Michael Bader
San Francisco, CA
www.michaelbader.com

More Than Bread and Butter/ Michael Bader -- 1st ed.

978-0-9962106-3-8

CONTENTS

FORWARD

Larry B. McNeil

Executive Director, Institute4Change

We welcome Michael Bader's book, "More Than Bread and Butter: A Psychologist Speaks to Progressives About What People Really Need In Order To Win And Change the World" as the first Institute4Change installment of a series of short books for serious progressives—organizers, leaders, activists, donors, and writers. Very rarely do we read something that changes the way we think. Even rarer is the book that propels us to act differently. "More Than Bread and Butter" is such a book. It slips up on you. Its honest and elegant simplicity calls us to question many of our assumptions about the human person, ourselves, the way we design and lead our organizations, and the way we win.

Though as a deeper journey into the human person it is not an attempt to be a primer for how to organize for social change, it will forever change how you think about yourself and the people you want to organize.

Exposure to the ideas in this book will hopefully help us understand the interior lives of people in a deeper and richer way than we previously imagined. Any of us who have successfully organized people for social change will recognize why we were successful. Those of us who have tried and failed will understand why we have failed.

What Dr. Bader makes compellingly clear is the cost of the mismatch today between what humans need and what most of our organizations provide. Simply put, progressives have built a series of organizations that routinely don't meet people's needs and, as a result, do not have the size, deep commitment, strategic discipline, or the flexibility to turn back a relentless right-wing and a venal .01 percent who are arrogantly twisting the world in their favor.

Dr. Bader challenges us to look deeper before we look wider, a direction that offers hope and possibility for a movement under constant attack and one needing fundamental repair.

Expanding the Vision of Progressive Leaders

I have the audacity to believe that peoples everywhere can have three meals a day for their bodies, education and culture for their minds, and dignity, equality, and freedom for their spirits.

—Martin Luther King Jr.

As progressives, we have a huge job in front of us in the fight for economic justice. But our leaders are trying to do their work with one hand tied behind their backs. The better ones may often do quite well fighting with one hand; many cannot. The problem and solution are more obvious than they think: *People become active in social-change movements because these movements speak to deep longings for meaning, recognition, relationship, and agency, as well as for economic survival and justice.*

The civil rights movement demanded basic economic and political equality. But it also spoke to a hunger to be connected to something bigger than the self. The institution that provided the base of this movement, the black church, grew and thrived on its power to provide meaning *and* recognition in dozens of way to its members. It provided meaning, in part, through the intense spirituality of its congregations, but also because it was wedded to a vision of social justice; recognition was afforded through the extensive social life in and around church life. The four girls killed in the bombing of the 16th Street Baptist Church in 1963 were on their way to give a performance, one of the many public ways that the church honored and recognized people in its community.

The women's movement initially based itself on the relational power of small groups. Pay equity and glass ceilings were important, yes; but second-wave feminism argued that personal *relationships*, and the needs, pleasures, and suffering they embodied, should also form the basis of a political agenda.

The highest periods of member engagement in the life of a labor union occur when people feel a sense of *agency* in standing up to a boss or during the height of a campaign. As Cesar Chavez observed, "The picket line is the best place to train organizers. One day on the picket line is where a man makes his commitment. … The picket line is a beautiful thing because it makes a man more human."

Survival needs aren't always primary

The power of human needs that go beyond the material would seem obvious. But progressive organizations instinctively and implicitly operate according to a "common sense" notion—one supported by researchers like Abraham Maslow, famous for his hierarchy or pyramid of human needs—that physical survival precedes those nonmaterial needs. This logic is simple: Without satisfying the basic needs for food, clothing, and shelter, people can't effectively address and gratify "higher" emotional, social, and spiritual needs. The strategic result is that we count on economic grievances and bread-and-butter issues like wages and benefits alone to move people to action.

But the compelling noneconomic needs for recognition, meaning, relationships, and agency can be sources of motivation every bit as powerful as survival needs. We see evidence of this every day. A terrorist commits suicide for the sake of Allah. An Indian demonstrator at a salt mine walks directly into the violent batons of the British Army in nonviolent resistance for the cause of independence; an African-American marcher sits down in front of Bull Connor's dogs. A marine risks his life for his buddy; a parent does the same for a child.

Everyone wants to earn money. But a great deal of research shows that people value meaning, connection, recognition, and agency as much as a bigger paycheck, and sometimes more. Many activists we've worked with in progressive organizations routinely give up higher-paying jobs in the private sector to work for social change. Even a lot of money can't always cure the deficit of other unmet needs. Paul Allen, co-founder of Microsoft, is currently worth $13 billion. Yet his autobiography prominently features his bitterness about being exploited by co-founder Bill Gates. Thirteen billion dollars did not make him feel good enough about the emotional conditions of his work.

Corporations and the Tea Party know more than we think

Bill Gates may not have gotten the message. But corporations have for decades understood the crucial motivational role of so-called soft needs apart from the paycheck. Almost every book on leadership published in the last 20 years emphasizes the importance of relationships and recognition. Huge studies have been done on companies that have succeeded and failed in their attempts to come up with the secret sauce of success and, invariably, these studies have found that success involves the ways that the culture of a company engages employees at levels above and beyond compensation. Soon after his retirement, Jack Welch, former CEO of General Electric, said, "My main job was developing talent. I was a gardener providing water and other nourishment to our top 750 people." Welch understood that personal development, not simply money, was the key to a successful company.

Even the exploitative world of advertising is increasingly recognizing that people aspire to more than just sex, money, and self-interest. The cutting edge of today's marketing strategies involve using "cause marketing" to appeal to consumers, often appearing first on social networking sites. Arianna Huffington, founder of the Huffington Post, is fond of citing an ad for Chivas Regal Scotch that begins with somber piano music, followed soon by the voice-over saying, "Millions of people, everyone out for themselves … can this really be the only way?" "No," the voice answers. "Here's to honor … and to gallantry." The commercial goes on to depict people helping someone push-start a broken-down car and tired firefighters after battling a blaze. "Here's to doing the right thing," the voice says, and to the "true meaning of wealth."

Blindness to these obvious needs is an important reason why the progressive movement is struggling today. So while the Left decries economic injustice and tries to organize campaigns against it, the response from the victims of injustice can be tepid. The Left helplessly watches as conservative megachurches, the evangelical movement, and the Tea Party draw people to communities that support a political and economic system that we see as inimical to their needs for material security. The reasons, though, have little to do with anyone's economic bottom line: These organizations and movements appear to address multiple levels of suffering and multiple needs.

Local Tea Party events honor the contributions of their organizers and encourage their creativity. Chapters often begin in someone's home and gradually include neighbors. Training and education are emphasized over and over. Further, their "us-against-them" mentality creates a (temporary) sense of community by scapegoating Obama, immigrants, liberals, and, as Mitt Romney so compassionately put it, the "47 percent." Megachurches engage their members in ways that speak to needs for recognition, connectedness, learning, and agency. They're growing. The progressive movement is struggling or even shrinking. It would be the height of denial to imagine that this is a coincidence.

You can't win hearts with "just the facts, ma'am"

In 2004, Republican strategist Karl Rove famously dismissed liberals as living in the "reality-based community," fuddy-duddies steeped in the delusion "that solutions emerge from the judicious study of discernible reality." Declared Rove: "That's not the way the world really works anymore." Was he ever right.

Because the *facts* of inequality are obvious and objectively measurable, we progressives believe that if we rationally present them, people will endorse our agenda. If we only had enough organizers and media to tell our story about class privilege, Wall Street and government corruption, and economic exploitation to working people, they'd see reality more clearly and want to join our movement. The implication is that "the people" are lacking knowledge or are suffering from what Marxists have called "false consciousness." Our job as progressives is to help people "see the light."

This assumption is empirically false and at odds with everything we know about psychology, learning, and neurobiology. Progressive strategists Anne Bartley and Al Yates have made this point by showing how progressive beliefs are grounded in American values, not simply intellectual beliefs. So has psychologist Drew Westen. Feelings matter, not facts. Values and noneconomic needs matter, not rational descriptions of economic reality. People have a range of desires and needs other than simple physical ones, and unless these desires and needs are understood and addressed, logic, facts, rationality, and education will all land on deaf ears.

Experts from other fields have also weighed in on this debate. University of California, Berkeley linguistics professor George Lakoff argues that people respond positively only to those messages that fit into deeply ingrained and pre-existing metaphors or frames through which everyone understands reality. These frames tend to refract experience. For example, the "facts" of economic suffering might, to the conservative, be interpreted as the moral failing of the victims, while to the liberal, it would reflect the failure of society and government to take care of them.

I recently had an email exchange with a conservative friend about the role of government spending and taxation in the current recession. I showed him lengthy analyses by economists Paul Krugman and Brad DeLong, who demonstrated that cutting taxes on corporate profits and on the incomes of the wealthy was a weak or even ineffective way of stimulating economic growth. My friend responded, "Krugman and DeLong are liberals ... of *course* they would say that!" For my friend, it was "case closed," not because of the facts, but because of his own values. Such biases trump objective truth every time.

Rather than walking around bewildered and frustrated that our apathetic or conservative fellow citizens are so stupid, progressives need to understand that the factual inequities of economic suffering are not adequate either to explain or change someone's potential for progressive political action. We have to see people's views in the context of their human needs and desires.

We are organizing the whole person—not just his or her pocketbook

This book seeks to change attitudes, not propose specific tactics. Its aim is to free us from our single-minded focus on the outrageous tragedy and crime of income inequality, as important as that issue might be, in order to begin to appreciate the whole person who works with and for us and whom we seek to engage.

It asks those of us in the progressive movement to re-examine our assumptions about what makes people tick, about what really matters to them and why. We need to examine our organizations and strategies in order to answer this question: Can we build progressive organizations around what people really need, thereby creating an institutional base with power, spirit, and energy? Does our movement—our visions, organizational structures, leadership styles, staff culture, political and growth strategies, public personas—embody a systematic appreciation of the full range of human needs?

Perhaps it is this instinct to see the whole person that has always accounted for the successes of great organizers. Our own hope is that a deeper understanding of human motivation will help create more great organizers and more success.

<u>Summary</u>

1) People become active in social-change movements because these movements speak to deep longings for meaning, recognition, relationship, and agency.

2) The common-sense notion that we need to satisfy people's material needs before we can speak to their psychological, social, and spiritual needs is wrong.

3) Both the private sector and the Right are better than progressives in speaking to people's noneconomic needs.

4) Feelings matter more than facts.

CHAPTER TWO

The Need to Survive: Beyond Economics

Definition: The need for economic security and the opportunity to acquire the basics of what Americans consider "the good life"

A wise man should have money in his head, but not in his heart.

—Jonathan Swift

If community, recognition, and meaning are so important, are we saying that people don't need material security and economic justice?

Of course not. Recognition doesn't put food on the table, and a sense of meaning won't stop the bank from foreclosing on your house. Addressing objective economic suffering and inequality have to continue to be centrally important in the progressive movement. The liberal belief in economic justice and a broader humanist vision of our collective obligation to provide a safety net for people unable to work or otherwise victimized by social and economic forces beyond their control has to remain a crucial core value.

These values ultimately focus on *survival needs*, not simply at the level of basic nutrition and shelter, but in terms of the need in all of us to have access to all the material benefits of the "good life" that should be afforded to people in an advanced industrial society. Survival, in other words, is not just basic material security.

When people's survival needs, defined in this way, are frustrated, the suffering that results is enormous. They get sick. In extreme cases, research shows that their brains actually atrophy as the result of deprivation. But it's not just bodies that suffer; spirits do too. People often internalize their "failure," blame themselves, and get depressed. They feel inadequate and inferior. They suffer from the meritocratic myth that their economic and material status is an expression of how deserving they are. A movement that doesn't speak directly to economic suffering and deprivation, whether absolute or relative, is going to not only be irrelevant to millions of people, but will take its place among other pie-in-the-sky movements, usually religious ones, that offer moral or spiritual bromides to the victims of material deprivation rather than directly seeking to end that deprivation.

A New Yorker cartoon succinctly captured this issue,

depicting a poor homeless man with a sign saying *"Need a Hug."* The humor of the cartoon comes from its absurdity. Economic and material suffering is a moral outrage in a society as wealthy as ours, and by addressing it—the fact of it, the injustice of it, and the real causes of it—we speak to a deeply important human need.

<u>Progressives, heal thyselves</u>

While we liberals and progressives champion economic security, there is one group we invariably forget about—ourselves. Progressive activists and organizers are too often martyrs. We fight for the "good life"—a living wage, health care, retirement security, the right to have leisure and a private life—for everyone but ourselves.

Beginning organizers in some of the largest and richest labor unions in the country rarely make much more than $30,000 per year. Regardless of experience and talent, organizers and leaders at all levels are expected to work constantly, sacrifice time that would otherwise be spent with their partners and children, shorten vacations or forgo them entirely, and be available 24/7 for the frequent crises that arise.

They sacrifice their health as well as their relationships. There is an extraordinarily high level of burnout and, therefore, of turnover. Absent the rewards of recognition and money that might induce people in the private sector to burn the candle at both ends, the motivation of progressives is supposed to come from their ideals. As one organizer told us, "I'm motivated by mission, not money." Later, she revealed that her stress-related asthma and tension headaches were gradually worsening and her son was having increasing troubles in school—both sources of great anxiety created by her version of "mission-driven" work.

My colleague Larry McNeil, a 25-year veteran of the Saul D. Alinsky Industrial Areas Foundation and, later, the executive director of the Institute4Change, puts a more organizational spin on this point. He argues that it takes five to seven years to develop a highly skilled organizer, one capable of building an organization from scratch and able to go into any situation and figure out how to win. When we work young people to death, he argues, we often get an unfortunate result—many of the better ones leave.

Guilt is a perverse motivator

Just as the Left has to recognize the positive emotional needs of working people, it not infrequently exploits the negative emotions of its own workers. Put plainly: The economic and physical deprivations of life on the Left rest much too heavily on a foundation of guilt. The guilt may often be unconscious, rearing its head in the willingness of staff to settle for crumbs when it comes to their own comfort and welfare while fighting for identical rewards for others. The need for more money, security, or leisure time is either subtly or overtly judged to be selfish—that those seeking to satisfy such needs are not "with the program," or "not committed." A culture develops that enforces self-denial and discourages or punishes perfectly normal needs for health and balance.

The cost of such antipathy toward survival needs is not only personal but organizational. Research shows that mastery of any professional practice—music, sports, leadership, organizing, teaching—requires many years of work, practice, and reflection. Therefore, our movement has to both change its relationship to the basic economic and survival needs of its members and create a financial base that allows for maturation and mastery. During the 1970s and 1980s, the United Farm Workers ignored its organizers' survival needs, paying them $5.00 a week. The toll on talented organizers was severe: divorces, alcoholism, and burnout. Many of the best people challenged the low salary scales and either quit or were fired.

Leisure is not a luxury

Too often hidden among the list of survival needs is the need for leisure. Human beings have a basic need to be "off"—not responsible, not performing—to craft a private life. In fact, there is abundant evidence that you can't be effectively "on" if you don't have time to be off. Research has shown, for example, that the daydreaming state is often responsible for our moments of greatest creativity.

The aphorisms we frequently hear today about the importance of "work/life balance" apply in spades to progressive leaders and activists. When an organizational culture forces people to work all the time, the symptoms of burnout begin to appear—illness, unclear thinking, a drift of focus toward the immediate results instead of long-range strategies, an implicit rewarding of simply "showing up" rather than performance, and more.

Burnout is sometimes thought to have three dimensions: *exhaustion, cynicism*, and a *lack of efficacy*. But exhaustion is not just the psychological and somatic damage inflicted by sleep deprivation. People may suffer from "compassion fatigue." They become cynical about their own values and vision for a better society. Their sense of personal agency declines.

On the other hand, when people take care of themselves, especially in their private lives and need for leisure, they become engaged and more effective. Studies have shown that performance diminishes when people work more than 50 hours a week; that breaks, time off, vacations, "down time"—different words for the same thing, really—are essential for maximum productivity and creativity. They restore healthy brain functioning, bolster the immune system, and mitigate mood swings.

When progressives talk about the importance of economic safety nets, support for working families, entitlements for people who need extra help, good holistic health care, and retirement security, we need to be sure we are looking inward as well as outward. Unfortunately, we often put ourselves on a cross of suffering, in order—ostensibly—to better fight to end the suffering of others. This is a bad bargain for all of the stakeholders in this fight.

Multiple human needs are universal

Too often, the organizers, activists, and leaders on the Left frame their work as being in the service of others. We're trying to help other people—the less advantaged, the powerless, the victimized. We fight for *their* right to leisure time but deny it to ourselves. We try to help *them* feel efficacious and inspired, but work for organizations that provide neither. In so doing, we often leave out ourselves. We deny that we have the same economic and noneconomic needs of those we're allegedly fighting for.

These needs are what it means to be human. They are universal. Their satisfaction can animate us to do good things and their unhealthy frustration can lead us to do bad things.

The human locomotive of need can drive us toward the light or the darkness. The question for progressives is whether or not we can get on board.

<u>Summary</u>

1) The liberal belief in economic justice and in a broader humanist vision of our collective obligation to provide a safety net for people unable to work or otherwise victimized by social and economic forces beyond their control is a crucial part of our core values and political agenda.

2) People internalize their economic insecurity and deprivations and blame themselves for being inadequate.

3) Leisure and reasonable limits on working hours prevent burnout and lead to greater engagement and productivity.

4) Progressives fight for others to have a right to the material rewards that make up the "good life" in America but regularly ignore their own needs because the culture of their organizations and their own psychology leads them to feel guilty about their own claims to more leisure, higher pay, and more work/life balance.

The Need for Meaning

Definition: The need for significance, to transcend one's individual ego, to contribute to and connect with something bigger than the Self

Those who have a "why" to live, can bear with almost any "how."

—Viktor Frankl

You're a British citizen. It's 1940. You turn on the radio and hear Winston Churchill as he makes this vow about Nazi aggression: *We shall fight in France ... We shall fight on the beaches ... We shall fight in the fields and in the streets, ... we shall fight in the hills ... we shall never surrender.*

It's late August in 1963. You're standing on the Washington Mall listening to Martin Luther King Jr.: *When we allow freedom to ring, when we let it ring from every village and every hamlet, from every state and every city, we will be able to speed up the day when all of God's children, black men and white men, Jews and Gentiles, Protestants and Catholics, will be able to join hands and sing in the words of the old Negro spiritual: Free at last! Free at last! Thank God Almighty, we are free at last!*

On a cold night in early January 2008, you turn on CNN and hear that Barack Obama has won in Iowa. You find yourself emotionally responding to this 46-year-old African American man as he speaks: *In the unlikely story that is America, there has never been anything false about hope.... It was a creed written into the founding documents that declared the destiny of a nation: Yes We Can. ... It was whispered by slaves and abolitionists as they blazed a trail towards freedom through the darkness of night: Yes We Can. ... And, together, we will begin the next great chapter in the American story with three words that will ring from coast to coast, from sea to shining sea: Yes We CAN!*

The contexts are radically different, but the intense emotions stirred in the audiences are similar. Great oratory summons up and makes political use of an intense longing in each of us for an experience of collective purpose, momentarily lifting us up out of our small individual selves and inviting us into something bigger, something transcendent. It is an intensely positive, even exultant, experience because a basic human need is being stimulated and gratified; *namely, the need for meaning.*

Research has shown that having purpose and meaning increases overall well-being and life satisfaction, improves mental and physical health, enhances resilience and self-esteem, and decreases the chances of depression.

Crises faced collectively generate meaning

The need to be connected to something bigger and grander than the self is immanent in our everyday lives, but especially manifest at times of crisis, struggle, and transformation. An activist in Madison, Wisconsin teared up as she recounted her experience during the February 2011 occupation of the State Capitol building and accompanying demonstrations that spontaneously erupted after Republican Governor Scott Walker took away collective bargaining rights for state workers. "I was wearing my orange vest," she said, "directing foot traffic, and during the course of my shift I saw my family doctor walk by, then my daughter's elementary school teacher, then an old childhood friend, and, finally, my mother!" She said that for some reason it reminded her of her favorite film, *It's a Wonderful Life*, in which the main character, a good and generous man named George Bailey, is rescued from despair by an unexpected outpouring of love from family, friends, and the broader community. This Wisconsin activist may have been working in her self-interest, defending her rights as a government worker, but she also felt—like George Bailey—part of something much bigger than herself and even bigger than her union. Community, solidarity, and love infused a mundane task—directing traffic—with meaning.

For labor unions, such needs come to the foreground at the beginning of every strike. The excitement and feeling of collective purpose, of being bigger than oneself, dominate the strikers. And that sense of purpose can be infectious. For example, in 2006, janitors in Chicago and New York City voted to support their fellow janitors who were then striking in Houston. Workers in Chicago and New York were willing to risk their own contracts to support people they'd never met because they were involved in a common struggle.

But if leaders elicit our longing for meaning as a *tactic*—a means to a political end—and then later ignore what they've elicited, it's not difficult to see how such longings can morph into cynicism, distrust, and anger. When our need for meaning is evoked through oratory alone, cynicism lies in wait. When it's evoked and reinforced in an on-going institution, it can have a powerful impact.

Several years ago, a large labor union hired a renowned design and innovation firm to enable it to understand how its members experienced their union. After embedding themselves with members for months, the consultants drew one powerful conclusion: Members felt connected to the union and to the higher purpose it represented during times of conflict. Between strikes and contract campaigns, however, this connection weakened, and member engagement radically decreased. If there was any relationship at all, it tended to be instrumental and contractual. In other words, the union only activated its members' passion at moments when members could readily see how their individual interests had to be subordinated to their collective one.

The challenge for progressive organizations is how to elicit and give voice to their members' need for meaning when there's *not* a crisis, a battle, an acute threat. Progressive organizations can't be "at the barricades" all the time even if they wanted to be.

Spiritual communities offer meaningful engagement

One place to look for examples of meaningful engagement is in religious and spiritual communities. If the need for meaning is a need for significance, a need to identify with something bigger than the individual self, then worshipping Jesus, Mohammed—God him/herself—represents the ultimate expression of meaning needs. As philosopher Paul Tillich put it, "Faith is an act of a finite being who is grasped by, and turned to, the infinite."

In addition, traditional religious institutions provide further outlets for the meaning needs of their members. Most religious congregations provide multiple vehicles for the satisfactions that come from helping others, from contributing to the community. Providing respite care, tending to the sick, organizing social events, etc., are all avenues for meaningful work that religious life offers its members. It both encourages and benefits from sponsoring and supporting the natural altruism—a powerful version of a meaning need—of human beings. In a recent study, sociologist Robert Putnam explains that "statistics suggest that even an atheist who happened to become involved in the social life of a congregation (perhaps through a spouse) is much more likely to volunteer in a soup kitchen than the most fervent believer who prays alone." Volunteerism, charity, committees offering succor and support, are all vehicles provided by many churches, synagogues, and mosques for the satisfaction of needs for meaning, as well as community.

Evangelical churches have systematic ways of inducting people into their communities by offering members opportunities to help others, to study and learn scripture, and to be part of something squarely on the side of the "mission" to which they've all been called. Is it any wonder a book that has sold more than 30 million copies, one written by megachurch pastor Rick Warren, is titled "The Purpose Driven Life"?

Twelve-step groups have saved thousands of lives not only because they invoke a "higher power" that helps addicts experience a bigger purpose, but because they strongly emphasize addicts' needs to transcend their own egos in service to other addicts; in other words, they elicit the need for meaning and purpose.

Religions can satisfy meaning needs by inspiring people to make sacrifices in their name, including sacrifices that can, unfortunately, do great harm. We have only to think of the Crusades, the Reformation, or the World Trade Center attacks to see the extent to which the need for spiritual meaning, when recruited to the service of baser ends, can be a frighteningly powerful force.

But if belief in God and spirituality can be used for bad purposes, it can certainly be used by radicals for good ones. In every religious tradition, there are powerful teachings, liturgies, and practices that mobilize meaning needs for progressive political change. Rabbi Michael Lerner, drawing from Jewish traditions, has shown how conceptions of God that involve the need for a strict and even punitive moral order exist alongside conceptions that emphasize compassion, love, justice, and freedom. Mahatma Gandhi, revered Indian advocate for the political power of nonviolence, speaking as a Hindu, had no problem integrating politics with his spiritual views, saying, "I could not be leading a religious life unless I identified with the whole of mankind, and that I could not do unless I took part in politics." And Christian activists are fond of citing those teachings attributed to Jesus that call for greater compassion for the poor and that critique the corruption of ruling elites.

The Left has always viewed religion as antithetical to the enlightenment values of reason, free inquiry, and open-mindedness. It suspects—often accurately—the Right of allowing into public life irrational beliefs that have either promoted intolerant or oppressive attitudes toward others or anesthetized people to their own oppression (Marx's "opium of the masses"). Notwithstanding the powerful example of the African-American civil rights movement, progressives today too often ignore, actively avoid, or are embarrassed by the experiences of meaning inherent in religious traditions.

This is a mistake. In our discomfort, we inadvertently comply with a tradition of assimilation in America; namely, that in exchange for protection from the type of persecution so common in the European countries from which people of faith came, religions here would be expected to maintain a strict division between private worship and political activity in the public sphere. As the Right challenges this division, the Left continues to uphold it, despite giving up an opportunity to connect with people's need for spiritual transcendence.

Work is about more than money

Since adults in the U.S. spend most of their waking hours at work, the office, factory, school, or other work sites are crucial arenas within which the need for meaning is either satisfied or frustrated. It is well-documented that corporate employees who are made to feel that they're contributing to something positive, something more than the company bottom line, feel motivated and good about their work. Even the janitors in an office building feel increased self-esteem when someone recognizes the contribution they make to the health and well-being of the buildings they clean.

Meaningful work is work in which people are engaged. If workers don't feel any sense of significance in what they do, if they lack support and an emotional connection of some kind to the outcome, they will not go the extra mile, and their employers will sacrifice productivity, performance, and face increased turnover.

In survey after survey, people list such subjective factors as recognition, the ability to do something that makes use of their talents, inclusion in decision-making, and friendly camaraderie as vital dimensions of workplace engagement. These factors are also correlated with mental health, reduced turnover, and even the company's productivity and bottom line. In the private sector, the opportunity to contribute to something bigger than the self might not involve politics, charity, or altruism, but instead "a quality product," "the customer," "safety," or even "the general public."

Material compensation is obviously important too, but employees' feelings about pay vary widely depending on whether noneconomic needs are being satisfied; if they aren't, then compensation rises in importance. Who was not moved by the sacrifice and heroism shown by the Japanese workers who remained at their damaged nuclear power plants in Fukushima? They risked their lives, not for money, but as an expression of their commitment to their jobs, their communities, and their country. Similarly, when firefighters rushed up the stairs at the World Trade Center on September 11, their sacrifice—one mirrored by other emergency workers there and in communities all across the country—had nothing to do with money or status, nothing to do with narrow self-interest, but instead, flowed from their self-image of providing service to their community, to something grander and nobler than their own egos or paychecks.

Such examples are dramatic but not rare. And yet progressives so often act as if these passions and motivations are incidental to the core interests of their constituencies.

Contributing to the future makes hardship bearable

Psychoanalyst Erik Erikson posited that in healthy middle age, there tends to be an emphasis on what he calls "generativity." For Erickson, generativity involves the need to make a difference, to contribute something to society. Among other things, generativity is often associated with the stage of raising children, fostering their trajectories out into the wider world. According to Erickson, its absence leads to struggles with meaninglessness and inactivity.

Thus, meaning needs lie behind a wide range of human activities that are experienced as contributing to "the future." The personal ambitions of artists, scientists, and intellectuals are often wedded to a need to contribute to something bigger than the self, to somehow make an enduring footprint that will last into the future. When an artist takes an internal vision and externalizes it onto a canvas, a musical score, or piece of clay, he or she is hoping to contribute it to the world, where it will have a perennial life of its own. One may write fiction because one "has to" express what's inside, but few writers don't also hope that their creative expressions will outlive them. It may be narcissistic for intellectuals to secretly believe their theories will forever change the way others think, but such grandiosity is also fueled by the need for meaning, to connect with and contribute to something larger, broader, and more significant.

And, of course, as Erikson argued, there is people's investment in children. A Chinese proverb says, "If you want happiness for a lifetime, help the next generation." In fact, working to ensure a better future for the next generation is so important that the pursuit of such an aim makes tolerable almost any degree of sacrifice and deprivation. Most Americans with children would say that the primary reward for working hard, for enduring the feelings of insecurity that plague so many people in their jobs, is the success of their children.

Psychiatrist Victor Frankl describes helping two suicidal men interred with him in a concentration camp during World War II. He urged them to consider that life was not done with them yet. To one, he emphasized a young son living abroad; to the other, a scientist, a series of books he needed to finish.

This implicit contract—I will work hard and suffer hardship to help my children have more than me—is currently being dashed by adverse economic conditions. With college and the promise of future success out of reach for increasing numbers of families, parents often cannot expect that their sacrifices will be redeemed in the next generation. The tragic frustration of the need—the meaning need—to provide a better life to one's children is at the heart of much of the anger and despair in middle- and working-class families today.

Political activism, even when its goals are practical and political, also can speak to this vision of contributing to the future through our children—a desire frequently described as being "part of history." During the struggle in Wisconsin, the Green Bay Press Gazette interviewed a protestor, Michele Brogunier, who said that she and her two daughters wanted to come to the rallies because they were concerned about their teachers. One even asked to stay the night in the Capitol, "so she could tell her grandkids about it." Another participant, Jim McKiernan, said his two grandnephews—one of whom carried a "Recall Walker" sign—were in awe of the spectacle. "This is history, man," said McKiernan, an instructor at Madison Area Technical College. "Hopefully we don't see this every generation, but it does seem like every one has these types of moments."

Meaning frustrated sours to cynicism

In the private sector, there is hardly an expert or study about leadership that doesn't emphasize the importance of leaders articulating a bold vision. Leadership guru Jim Collins argues that a well-conceived vision both emphasizes core values and audaciously envisions an inspiring future. If our leaders cannot articulate a vision of what their people and organizations can be, they can't paint a picture of a reality radically bigger than the current one. They/we become stuck in what Larry McNeil calls the "eternal present."

The flight from vision—from possibility—frustrates people's hunger for meaning and purpose. The result is resignation and cynicism. Yet leaders are constantly stepping back from the visionary to the mundane, back from what could be to what is, no matter how miserable the status quo. Barack Obama stimulated and began to gratify the need for meaning during his 2008 campaign by articulating a vision of compassion, justice, and hope. But as soon as he took office, the president and his "savvy" insiders switched the channel back to the familiar one dominated by practical economic legislation and the needs they addressed, inside-the-Beltway compromises, and the media-driven competition to define the message of the day. Obama's ability to tap into our aspirations and need for a grander purpose was unfortunately matched by his turn to the discourse of *realpolitik*.

Then in 2010, when his former passionate supporters couldn't generate much enthusiasm around the midterm elections, Obama was irritated. He appeared to share the cynical wisdom that those who still longed for something more transcendent were naive idealists. That attitude just increased people's disaffection: Cynicism derives not only from disappointment and the experience of hopes repeatedly dashed, but also from the embarrassment of having ideals deemed "unrealistic."

Long ago, Hillary Clinton also learned the lesson that idealism is "naive" and cynicism "realistic." Playing on the words of Oscar Wilde's observation that "the cynic is a man who knows the price of everything but the value of nothing," Mrs. Clinton once declared that "the *market* knows the price of everything but the value of nothing." She went on to say, "We need a politics of meaning" in America. When the press found out that a Left-wing rabbi was articulating the same concept, they had a field day mocking Clinton for spouting spiritual gobbledygook.

Like any savvy politician, Clinton backed away from this message. The problem wasn't that she took the politically safe and strategically smart path in this instance., it was simply that, in the world of politics, "soft" messages about meaning and purpose—especially when used to critique the ways that the market demeans us—are immediately scorned and punished.

Cynicism can be private or public

Moving from the macroclimate of politics to the microworld of the individual, these same basic dynamics are clearly visible. As a psychologist, the heart of the mental suffering I see in my consulting room is nothing more than another form of cynicism; namely, the unconscious belief that *the way things are is the way they're supposed to be.* The essential elements of this belief are: 1) the pursuit of normal and healthy goals, or the expression of healthy feelings, will be psychologically dangerous because they may endanger important relationships; 2) that this danger will take the form of unbearable feelings of loss, fear, shame, or guilt; and 3) that the safest route forward therefore involves giving up the desired goal or suppressing the normal feeling.

My patient Lisa grew up in a family in which her anxious and hypochondriacal mother couldn't take care of her. Lisa inferred that this was normal and, further, that her own needs to be cared for burdened her mother. When she carried this belief into her adult life, she found that it was confirmed by partners or friends who seemed to have little bandwidth to listen to Lisa's problems. Her cynical assumption that others would be burdened by her feelings and needs was mirrored by real experience.

I helped Lisa in two ways: First, I helped her understand the origins and workings of her painful (and false) inferences and beliefs; and, second, as a result of my own attitude of acceptance and caretaking, I provided her a direct and powerfully disconfirming experience within our therapy relationship.

Like cynics everywhere, Lisa did not consider herself a cynic. Instead, her symptoms felt entirely *realistic* to her.

Cynics generally call themselves realists. Unfortunately, cynicism tends to generate beliefs that confirm and reflect aspects of reality that then mirror and reproduce the cynical sensibility. Invariably, the reality that is experienced features only the basest of human motivation. It's a perfect self-reinforcing loop—not a mirror, but a hall of mirrors.

In the political arena, the underlying assumptions of much of the populace—spoken or not—are that everyone is out for themselves, no leader can be trusted, people want to line their pockets at others' expense, no one in positions of authority really cares about ordinary people, and the only people who are trustworthy are in our own families—and then only barely. That these assumptions often turn out to be true in no way negates their inherent distortion. In reality, people—including politicians—are complicated, wanting to do good and compelled to do bad, honest and dishonest, altruistic and self-centered. Cynicism reduces a complex reality to a simple and negative one. Moreover, cynicism dictates that people and the world can't really change.

The 24-hour news media—and we as its viewers—deny the truth that people are complex. For example, we all assume that when a politician shows up at a natural disaster, he or she is posing, performing, posturing. Determined never to appear gullible or to mistake the performance for reality, reporters and newscasters cover these performances *as* performances. So convinced are they that politics is *only* about performance, in fact, that when a public figure feels and expresses a genuine, heartfelt, unedited sentiment, reporters can't perceive or believe in it. They report on this authentic emotion "objectively"— telling us only how it "plays" politically.

You get what you ask for—ask for little, get little

I have led countless workshops with progressive leaders to help them expand their notions of their staffs' and members' needs to include connection, meaning, recognition, and agency. I often solicit examples of such desires from their own lives and work. Invariably, someone raises a hand and says, with some frustration or heat, "This is all well and good, but we want to also be sure that we don't get too touchy-feely when we're dealing with our members and the media."

My standard response, usually successful in eliciting audience laughter, is something like, "Look, I want to reassure you: You are in no danger of becoming too touchy-feely. In fact, if you sat on a mountaintop and contemplated your navel for a year, you would barely move the dial on the "touchy-feely meter!"

Humor aside, the issue goes to the heart of cynicism. "Touchy-feely" is a disparaging term applied to unwanted sentiment, open displays of emotion, physical closeness, or excessive empathy. If you or your attitude is "touchy-feely," it's probably soft, weak, not serious or tough. Organizing and politics, on the other hand, are supposed to be hard-edged. They're supposed to be about "real" things—money, time, working conditions—not airy intangibles like meaning or connection. The thinking goes, "If we don't feature and fight for bread-and-butter issues, people won't believe that we're truly progressive and certainly won't be willing to get more actively engaged."

The problem with this thinking is if we treat people as if they are primarily consumers interested in their own selfish bottom line, people see the same values in us and respond accordingly. We ask them only for what we think they'll give, and they give us what they think we need. Cynicism becomes "normal." And the distorted belief that transformative change is impossible becomes "realistic."

We can face reality and also address the need for meaning

Progressive organizations today, however, tap into little of this energy. They don't put forth a vision that truly excites large numbers of people—instead, reworking and regurgitating liberal mottos of the '60s and '70s about economic fairness and about providing a safety net and justice to people at the bottom of the economic totem pole. Noble, compelling, and, for liberals and progressives, core values, for sure. But even people at the bottom don't find such values particularly compelling because they have internalized their own economic failures into a well of private despair, or, if not, have cynically retreated to a political passivity that greets every messenger from the Left with "what have you done for me lately?" rather than "what can I do to be part of this exciting movement?" If the only vision that progressives have to offer is one based on what was called "The American Dream"—the basis of the economic growth of the middle class following World War II—then the response will tend to be either apathy or cynicism.

The Right foments cynicism about some things and an almost-religious faith about others. Ironically, it elicits cynicism by satisfying a deep need for meaning. The Tea Party invites people to come out of the private spaces in which they suffer economic anxieties and helpless frustration into a public space with a ready-made community, purpose, and, most important, an enemy waiting for them. It validates people's cynical belief that huge anonymous forces like government (note: not corporations) collide with them in ways that render them helpless. At the same time, it offers them ideals and images that give them a sense of being connected to something great, something perfect, something worth fighting for. That's why some

Tea Partiers walk around with copies of the Constitution in their pockets or like to quote the founders. These are the symbols of an ideal state of being that liberals have irreparably tarnished but that must command absolute reverence.

By reinforcing people's cynicism about government, the Right seeks to stir up feelings of righteousness about its role and movement.

Whether or not its tactics are manipulative, the Right is sophisticated in mobilizing passionate engagement by speaking directly to people's needs for connection and high ideals.

The "middle-class dream" that progressives offer up cannot pierce people's despair because it does not speak to anything beyond the desire, however strong, for the adequate satisfaction of material needs—enough, for example, to buy a home, send your kids to college, and retire. It's true that such a vision also speaks to desires for security, family, and health. But when progressives privilege economic security above all other needs, they do more than shoot their capacity for inspiration in the foot. They also implicitly posit a view of "the good life" that is dangerously incomplete and distorted.

By that I mean that, even among the demographic strata (mostly white and middle class) actually *living* the American Dream following World War II, enormous suffering bubbled under the surface. This suffering had a great deal to do with the spiritual, psychological, and cultural deprivation that marked that period in America. An army of sociologists, psychologists, and cultural critics began to notice that the "good jobs" of the '50s were also *alienated* ones, shot through with anxiety and powerlessness. Affordable public education was based on mindless conformism. Homes could be owned, but suburbanization separated neighbors from neighbors, and children from grandparents. The "living wage" that unions fought so hard for was presumed to apply only to men, and women were supposed to celebrate their domesticity and responsibility for raising children in increasingly isolated nuclear families.

Sexual hypocrisy, Cold-War paranoia, conspicuous consumption, the breakdown of extended families and communities—the list could go on. It was a form of suffering memorialized in numerous books and films, from "The Man in the Gray Flannel Suit" to Betty Friedan's "Feminine Mystique," the book that coined the phrase, "the problem that has no name"—the silent despair of isolated housewives—and helped provide one of the stimuli for consciousness-raising groups and the burgeoning feminist movement. Let's remember that, despite their excesses and political naiveté, the '60s generation was rebelling against something *real*.

I am *not* arguing that a movement that promises people jobs, health care, and economic security will fall on deaf ears because these needs are unimportant. I am saying that promises of more money and equity can't come close to providing a vision or strategy that will engage people in our movement.

I am saying that the activists leading a progressive movement as well as the people they hope to engage in it over the long haul are much more than consumers of material goods and services. They are animated by multiple needs and longings. The only way they will do more than write a check or pull a voting switch is if these needs and longings are named and addressed: if the politics and vision of the Left offer them *meaning.*

Summary

1) The need to be connected to something bigger and grander than the self is deeply embedded in our everyday lives.

2) Meaning is often found in spiritual communities. Because of its fear of Right-wing attacks on the separation of church and state, the Left insufficiently speaks to the ways that spirituality is embedded in universal meaning needs and can, therefore, potentially serve progressive ends.

3) Meaning needs can be found in social movements, work, artistic and intellectual work, and in our relationship to our children and to the next generation.

4) In the absence of a vision of the future that speaks to people's meaning needs, the result is cynicism.

5) The economically based "middle-class dream" is no longer inspiring enough to politically engage masses of people.

CHAPTER FOUR

The Need for Relationship

Definition: The need to be connected to others in ways that involve mutuality and reciprocity.

We are all so much together, but we are all dying of loneliness.

—Albert Schweitzer

Collective bargaining, picket lines, demonstrations, "cells," consciousness-raising groups, online Twitter-based demonstrations—progressives have grasped the power of relationships since the dawn of social- change movements. People join such movements not only to achieve important political ends but also for the opportunity to connect with others.

The need for social connection, including intimate attachments, is universal. We're born with the need and capacity for it; it is hard-wired in our brains. In a New Yorker cartoon depicting two birds on a tree branch, one bird says to the other, *"Of course I love you. I'm programmed to love you. I'm a goddamn lovebird!"* The same could be said for humans.

Attachment sustains us physically and psychologically throughout our lives. Without it, we get depressed, detached, and lonely. In our search for it, we will climb any mountain, ford any stream, suffer any abuse, and take any risk. The increasing absence of attachment in contemporary life has been decried by psychologists and sociologists alike. Its various distortions underlie most forms of psychopathology, and its vital presence accounts for the healing power of psychotherapy.

<u>"Us vs. them" has no political allegiance</u>

And yet, as opportunities for social relatedness decline, as Americans—to quote sociologist Robert Putnam—increasingly "bowl alone," it is not the Left but the Right that has stepped up to fill this unmet need. The success of megachurches, for example, owes more to the ways they encourage connectedness than in their spiritual persuasiveness. In a September 2005 New Yorker article titled "The Cellular Church," Malcolm Gladwell explained the phenomenal growth of pastor Rick Warren's Saddleback Church in just these terms. The real work—both spiritual and organizational—of Warren's church takes place in groups of seven to eight people who meet weekly to pray, offer mutual support, and volunteer for broader church projects. The large size of the congregation rests on a dense relational base.

As the Communist Party understood in the '30s, the women's movement in the '60s and '70s, and 12-step groups today, small groups are an especially powerful means to provide comfort, exert influence, and promote growth because they speak directly to the human need for connection.

In fact, if we begin with the assumption that people have a compelling need to belong, to be connected to each other as part of a community, then political movements that exaggerate an "us" versus "them" mentality will speak to this need more than a movement that challenges the irrationality of inequality. Conservative communities tend to do the former. Tea Partiers defending the Constitution against government intrusion; the NRA defending its homes against criminals and its right to bear arms against liberal gun control advocates; Christians threatened by gay marriage; whites threatened by scary depictions of Muslims and foreigners; elderly people threatened by rapidly changing customs—all are answering the call to be safely attached to a virtuous community, a comforting "us" imperiled by outside threats from a bad "them." Unfortunately, these forms of community require the demeaning and demonization of some other group.

The Left can and does also demonize the "other." We tend to feel a distinct lack of compassion and understanding for our political enemies, fueled often by projections that help us sustain *our* sense of connectedness and specialness. However, while we often exhibit similar dynamics, progressives believe that the demeaned "other"—racists, sexists, Tea Partiers, anti-government fanatics, etc.—are threatening values that are objectively moral, values like compassion, social justice, equality, and mutual recognition. Furthermore, the Left doesn't tend to hate and want to hurt our enemies in the same way that the Right does.

The history of social-change movements is the history of conflicts in which organizers intentionally foster relationships, community, and a feeling of being part of a common group fighting for a common goal. Labor unions formed and grew not just because their members shared common economic interests but because organizers helped workers see that they were not alone, that they were part of something larger, a group that shared collective pain and potentially collective power, and that this community of interests was in direct conflict with those of their bosses. The women's movement was grounded in similar dynamics, emphasizing the common experience of women suffering at the hands of a common enemy—sexist, patriarchal men.

The world was riveted by scenes from Cairo's Tahrir Square when ordinary Egyptians stood up to the power of a dictator on behalf of freedom. Interviews with the participants rarely focused on economic deprivation as the motivation behind their risky public displays. Instead, their passion had to do with meaning, with agency, and with community. Ahmed Abdel Reheem, a 40-year-old electrician from Alexandria who gave up his monthly income of $200 and camped out in the downtown square for weeks, put it this way: "All I cared about before was making a living, but now people have started to care about each other. I feel like I have been born again."

These gratifying effects of connectedness don't discriminate on the basis of political orientation. My father tells stories of being in uniform, home on leave during World War II, and going into bars where he couldn't buy his own drink because of the huge public support of the war and the American soldiers and sailors fighting it. My mother had a victory garden, saved scrap metal, and sold war bonds. The sense of community, of being united for a "good cause," was palpable in the U.S. during World War II. And yet the need that this experience stimulated and gratified is identical to the one gratified now in the training camps of Right-wing survivalist militias in Idaho for whom the common enemy isn't Germany or Japan, but the U.S. government itself.

Thus, the need for relationships can be satisfied in ways that promote either progressive political change or regressive conservative reaction. The longing for community can be gratified in a gang or a co-op, a lynch mob or a hunger strike, a rally for Sarah Palin or Barack Obama. What is clear is that its satisfaction creates a powerful bond and potential foundation for political action.

Relationships are a matter of life and death

In the '30s and '40s, orphanages in Britain reported a high incidence of a syndrome that came to be called "failure to thrive." Despite being well fed, clothed, and housed, many orphaned babies and toddlers failed to develop, lost weight, became ill, and sometimes died. Esteemed psychological investigators like Rene Spitz and John Bowlby showed that the problem lay in the absence of a secure attachment, a relationship that in the earliest months and years could only be established through touch, cuddling, holding, rocking, and eye contact. In Britain's wartime orphanages, or "foundling homes," as they were called, many illnesses and distress were alleviated when caretakers were coached to pick children up and simply hold them. There was enough food, but the environment's failure to feed the hunger for connection had been life-threatening.

The physiological and medical consequences of attachment and/or its absence are now well known. Loneliness—the absence of significant emotional attachments—is associated with a wide range of physical ailments. Director of the Center for Cognitive and Social Neuroscience at the University of Chicago John Cacioppo, Ph.D. and other researchers have found that loneliness is correlated with greater resistance to blood flow through the cardiovascular system, higher levels of the stress hormone cortisol, altered gene expression in immune cells, impaired sleep, and a faster progression of Alzheimer's disease. Elderly people lacking social interaction are twice as likely to die prematurely. Good marriages extend the life expectancy of both men and women, while bad marriages reduce it, and the loss of a spouse is one of the best predictors of premature death, especially in men.

And these are consequences of a condition that is getting worse in our society. Research shows that people have fewer friends and confidantes than they did 20 years ago. The average household size is decreasing. In 2013, over 30 percent of Americans lived alone, up from 17 percent in 1970. In a recent survey, 40 percent of adults said that they were lonely, double the number reported in the 1980s. Cacioppo and others argue that loneliness should rank with smoking as a public health risk.

Internet-based relationships are a double-edged sword in their effect on loneliness and disconnectedness. On the one hand, most users say that they are in regular contact with a much wider and more varied network of friends and family than ever before. On the other hand, many of these contacts are superficial—people portraying themselves in ways closer to how they'd like to be seen rather than who they are. And, of course, it's impossible to walk down almost any American city nowadays and not notice how many people are utterly unaware of their natural and social environment because they are glued to their smartphones. I recently attended a Major League baseball game and sat behind a group of five teenage girls. Every one of them spent most of the game texting each other and friends. A recent cartoon captures this phenomenon perfectly. A rather nerdy young adult, computer open in front of him (or her), is on the phone saying, "A bunch of friends are coming over to stare at their phones."

The need for relationships is not some "soft" need, but one central to our physical and emotional well-being. It is hard-wired. Babies are born adapted to connect to their mothers, and mothers are hormonally and psychically primed to reciprocate. When attachment needs are frustrated, we suffer. Still, we hold on for dear life. We desperately try to adapt, even if it means hurting ourselves. It is well known that children regularly choose to stay with an abusive caretaker rather than face the loss of that person to whom they are attached. In their minds, a bad relationship is better than no relationship. To face the reality of a caretaker's failure would mean surrendering the illusion of care and the imaginary connection underneath it. And an illusion is better than nothing.

For this reason, it is often said of children that they would rather be "sinners in heaven than saints in hell." The child's unconscious, but false, belief is that if only he or she were better or different, the parent(s) would treat him or her better as well.

Loneliness is not our own fault

Such longing and self-blame are obviously not limited to children. In a recent article in Slate magazine about loneliness, author Jessica Olien reports how frequently she heard people report thinking, "If I were a better person, I wouldn't be lonely." Many an adult patient has told me that a bad relationship is preferable to being alone. Men in particular often grow up isolated because they are trapped within a gender role that views a dependency on or desire for relationships as weak. This emotional disconnectedness often underlies the turn by men to Internet-based erotic relationships that promise to safely, albeit momentarily, slake their thirst for relationship. Whether inhibited, sublimated, or openly expressed, the desire for what philosopher Martin Buber called "I-Thou" relationships—relationships based on reciprocity and mutual recognition—is everywhere.

Talk to any therapist about the worst traumas he or she treats and about how his or her patients get better. Over and over again, you will hear that severe neglect, emotional absence, or an inconsistent or undependable parental presence creates the worst damage in a developing child. And over and over again, you will hear therapists admit that the healing process depends more on the quality of the relationship between the therapist and the patient than on the brilliant theory-driven interpretations of the therapist. Because people are wounded and derailed in their development by unhealthy relationships, their "cure" derives in large part from the ability of the therapist to provide healthy emotional experiences in the therapeutic relationship that correct what was damaged. Bad relationships hurt; good relationships heal.

In the 1980s, researchers conducted a famous experiment that led them to conclude that drug addiction was a function of the compelling effects of the drug itself. They put a rat in a cage that provided two sources of water, one of which was laced with cocaine. The rat preferred the cocaine-laced water to such a degree that it drank until it died. However, in 1980, psychology professor Bruce

Alexander of Canada's Simon Fraser University had already published a study that, while overlooked, directly challenged this particular view of addition. Alexander constructed an experimental environment he called "Rat Park," a lush cage with several rats, which provided interesting things to explore, and great rat food. He found that in enriched and intensely social environments such as Rat Park, the rats shunned the cocaine-laced water and none died. He concluded that the opposite of addiction was not sobriety, but social connection.

In the course of working with patients of all classes, races, ages, and diagnoses, I am struck by how often I encounter the scourge of loneliness in even the most successful of them. Over and over, people tell me about the private suffering and sense of isolation that stem from an inability to be authentically themselves. They tell me how much their lives are consumed by performing numerous roles, fashioning different selves, and desperately seeking to please others even at the cost of not pleasing themselves. I'm not talking here about the normal sociability that ordinary human communities require, a sociability that naturally involves intuiting what other people need, how they feel, and what is required to get along with them. I'm not, in other words, talking about normal adaptation, but, instead, a type of adaptation many of us have made to social expectations and to environments that aren't interested in or capable of understanding and appreciating who we really are. And when we adapt to something pathological, that pathology comes to feel like a normal part of ourselves and the world.

My patient Katherine was one such person. She was a mother, wife, and co-owner with her husband of a family business. She was a daughter, sibling, and friend. Her life seemed full and gratifying. Except that Katherine felt invisible in almost every one of these relationships. She was around others a lot but felt alone. Why? Because Katherine's need for connection—like the need for connection in all of us—was not satisfied simply by the physical presence of others. Instead, she needed to feel that she was important to others for who she was, and not simply for what she could do for them. She needed to feel that the people close to her *saw* her. And she didn't feel any such thing.

Katherine is an example of the overlap of many of her noneconomic needs. The perceived failure of others to understand her made her feel cut off and disconnected, thereby frustrating her need for deeper and more satisfying relationships.

Katherine had grown up in a family in which invisibility was the norm: Children, her parents said, should be seen and not heard. In their defense, her parents were overwhelmed in their own lives and had little energy left for Katherine. Moreover, her siblings, unfortunately, were competitors for scarce resources, and were not fraternal and loving peers. So Katherine held the false but understandable belief that she wasn't supposed to need mutuality, that the only safe way of guaranteeing secure connections to others was to facilitate and gratify *their* needs. This conditioned her choice of mates and friends, all of whom tended to be self-centered.

Now imagine if Katherine was someone we wanted to organize. She'd probably give us some money or show up to a phone-bank on Election Day if she believed enough in the cause. But what if we really connected with her, displayed genuine curiosity in who she was and what she felt? What if we were interested in discovering her deepest aspiration and found her a more meaningful role doing important work that reflected those aspirations? We would be counteracting or "disconfirming" her most painful belief. We would be speaking to her deepest longing. And we would then potentially be able to engage her deepest passions.

Forming relationships is the core of political organizing

If attachment is necessary for psychic growth and even physical survival, it is no wonder that the task of forming relationships should be the central task of a political organizer. A simple conversation in which another person feels understood and connected creates the psycho-social-biological foundation for a possible political association around common interests. It creates a relationship, a bond that potentially leads to trust and openness to various forms of engagement. When the person being organized senses, however, that he or she is simply a means to an end—not *really* someone intrinsically interesting to the organizer—then the relationship will be empty or non-existent, and invariably fail to generate real political engagement. When the father of community organizing, Saul Alinsky, made individual meetings and house meetings the center of his organizing approach, he—like all great organizers—understood that it is only through relationships, often established one by one through simple conversation, that people feel enough trust to begin to articulate their real needs and join with others in collective political action.

In an October 2010 New Yorker article titled, "Small Change," Malcolm Gladwell made a similar point about the relational basis of political organizing by retelling the story of the Greensboro Four, the four African-American students who attempted to integrate a segregated lunch counter in 1960. On the first day, there were four students, and these four were close friends and colleagues in the burgeoning desegregation movement in that area. The second day, there were 31 students there, most from the same dormitory. On subsequent days, the crowd swelled to 80, then 300, and then 600. Gladwell's point is that this crowd developed rapidly, not with the use of modern social media like Twitter or Facebook, but through a grapevine of dense relationships based in schools and local churches. It was the presence of personal relationships that enabled these four students to take risks, and that provided the engine for growth and political power.

We need to learn how to talk to each other

Most political leaders and organizers will agree that relationship building is the sine qua non of their work. However, in our many years of working intensively with political leaders and organizers, we've found that many were alarmingly poor at having simple relational conversations. We had several training sessions in which organizers would be asked to pair up and have a 10-minute conversation, the instruction for which was simply to "begin to form a relationship." Often, even the most experienced leaders had difficulty. They entered conversations with an "ask" in mind, something they wanted to get the other person to do. Or else they wanted to "fix" or "solve" the other person's problems. They listened only to the words and not the music, the possible underlying meanings that often lie behind spoken content. And instead of asking the other person to clarify things they didn't understand, they imposed their own assumptions of what was meant. They had a hard time being curious, and they couldn't be vulnerable or self-disclosing in any way. While they initially argued that these failures were a function of the artifice of the exercise, eventually it became clear that these problems riddled their everyday interactions with members.

In our view, this difficulty getting into genuine relationship with real and potential followers and constituencies is one of the many reasons that so many people don't vote or otherwise engage in the public political world. Many or even most of our constituencies don't believe that we are interested in them as people. The relationship is instrumental. We want their votes, their money, and their time. No wonder people are too often ambivalent about giving us any of these things, much less actively engaging in the movement we're trying to build.

We suppose that union organizers and leaders, more than most progressives, understand the power of collective action, and yet apart from discrete and infrequent periods of high conflict—such as contract time or strikes— these organizers and leaders "forget" that the need for connectedness persists in the background, all the time. It is a need likely being met, at least to some degree, by family and friendship networks, if not by institutions like conservative organizations, churches, sports teams, and civic organizations— everywhere, you might say, *but* in the union. Gone are the days of the "union hall" that sponsored activities bringing members and their families together, or that otherwise sought to constitute a community. During peacetime, such avenues for solidarity and community have disappeared from people's lives as a vehicle for connection.

Still, to the extent that progressives continue to ignore the centrality of attachment and the need for reciprocity and relatedness in their members—in their work, in their relationship to their union, and in their public life—the vacuum that this oversight creates will be filled by the other side.

Disasters and revolutions have something in common

Some leaders argue that such needs for connection are and should be more appropriately met in our private lives. But the need for connection and community is much larger than romantic love and family. People like working in teams. They like being fans with other fans at musical and sporting events. They feel connected—for better or worse—to their hometowns, to their companies, to their races, their religions, and their nations.

Ask any organizer whether he or she would prefer to work alone or with someone else—the answer is almost always the latter. Staff of progressive organizations need to be in relation to each other just as much as they need to be in relation to the people they're organizing. If members wrestle with isolation or loneliness, so do staff. And yet attending to such needs too often takes a back seat to the "real" work of the union—fighting the boss, handling grievances, and bargaining for more money. Staff resources are stretched thin. Cultivating connection doesn't seem to be on the to-do list.

Still, examples abound that should reassure progressives that things could be otherwise. Whether you think it's a good strategy or not, we can get lots of people to a demonstration. If the cause is right, that demonstration can evoke and express the energy freed up when individuals find themselves part of a meaningful group. Those of us who have felt that energy—anyone who has been actively involved in the civil rights, LGBT, anti-war, anti-nuke, women's, or, most recently, Occupy movements—know it can become one of the most gratifying experiences of one's life.

Again, the research is compelling on this point. Two needs intersect in the experience of working—or demonstrating—with other people. When the need for affiliation and connectedness is met, people also experience a greater sense of meaning and purpose.

In her book, A Paradise Built in Hell: The Extraordinary Communities that Arise in Disaster, journalist and activist Rebecca Solnit argues that, however temporary, natural disasters open powerful channels for the experience of belonging, community, and meaning. She studied the responses of communities hit by disasters, ranging from two devastating earthquakes in San Francisco and one in Mexico City; the catastrophic explosion of the Norwegian ship, the Imo, in Halifax, Canada, in 1917; various floods and heat waves; the September 11, 2001 attacks on the World Trade Center; and the near-destruction of large swaths of New Orleans by Hurricane Katrina in August 2005.

Her findings are profound and provocative. She found that, following disasters, most ordinary people reacted in altruistic ways, urgently engaged in caring for themselves and those around them, strangers and neighbors, as well as friends and loved ones. Contrary to the "official" or media-driven expectations that such radical disruptions in the social order would likely result in chaos, disorder, and criminality, the evidence is otherwise. In each of the disasters that Solnit studied, there were not only extraordinary acts of individual heroism, but countless small efforts by the people affected to help each other, to assume enough agency to establish order and recreate their own version of what Martin Luther King Jr. called the "beloved community"—an integrated society, a community of love and justice wherein brotherhood (and sisterhood) would be an actuality in all of social life.

The result was often exhilaration rather than despair. Of course, Solnit is not ignoring the tremendous suffering that also resulted from these disasters, nor the presence of criminality and cruelty. Her point is that, contrary to the beliefs of elites and authorities that major social and physical disruptions would free the selfish beast in people, disasters, instead, seemed to free up deep longings and capacities for mutuality, altruism, and attempts to actualize these values in various forms of mutual aid. People became creative in their search for ways to help each other, deriving as much satisfaction from improvising ways of helping as did the recipients of such help. When the ordinary divisions between people were smashed, people regularly became their "brothers' keepers." Her book is replete with hundreds of such examples, big and small.

Solnit makes a clear distinction between these forms of altruism that express the need for connection and meaning, and charity. The former reaches across the divides that separate us with solidarity and empathy, while the latter "gives" from a high altitude, from the top down. Solnit is talking about human nature, about what makes people tick when catastrophes collapse traditional patterns of competition and isolation, and people's innate needs for community and a sense of being connected to something bigger than the self are suddenly freed up. Solnit's examples, similar to those associated with explicit rebellions against the status quo, reflect the importance of connection and relationship in the public—not private—sphere, and expressed in action and not simply in the heart. She sums up her main thesis this way: "The history of disaster demonstrates that most of us are social animals, hungry for connection, as well as for purpose and meaning. It also suggests that if this is who we are, then everyday life in most places is a disaster …"

The real question is: How do we translate the emotional power and enthusiasm liberated by the collective action resulting from either radical politics or natural disasters into ongoing political work that depends on organization and builds enduring political power? That question is not the same as, "How do we activate people to fight from time to time for their own interests?" Rather, it is, "How do we *sustain over the long haul* the energy and solidarity generated by huge public events?" How do we use the tropism of human beings toward belonging to build a movement that is powerful, effective, gratifying, and (dare we say it?) joyful for everyone in it?

Organizers often say to us, "You're talking pie-in-the-sky here. People don't want to relate to us in any way *other* than the way they already do. It's just common sense!" Our response is this: *You deliver what you imagine people ex-*

pect, and people expect what they think you're able to de-liver. To the extent that progressives continue to ignore the centrality of attachment and the need for reciprocity and relatedness in people they want to organize—in their work, in their relationship to progressive organizations, and in their public life—the vacuum that this oversight creates will be filled by the other side.

Summary

1) The need for social connection is universal. We're born with it and it is hard-wired in our brains.

2) Loneliness and disconnectedness are often such painful experiences for both children and adults that we would do almost anything to avoid it.

3) As people in our society become more isolated and lonely, the Right has an opening to provide what is missing from people's lives.

4) The history of progressive and radical movements has always created or emphasized opportunities for greater feelings of community.

5) The experience of disaster often opens doors to unmet longings for mutuality, meaning, altruism, and community.

CHAPTER FIVE

The Need for Recognition

Definition: The experience of being seen and understood as unique and special

There are two things people want more than sex and money: recognition and praise.

—Mary Kay Ash, founder of Mary Kay Cosmetics

All people need to be seen as unique and special. When this need is satisfied, psychologists call the result "healthy narcissism" (to be distinguished from the selfish grandiosity implied in the complaint, "That person is so narcissistic!") Healthy narcissism, or positive self-esteem, results when the normal need for recognition is met in the course of development. It builds up a person's capacity to meet life's challenges with confidence. If this need is not met, the person becomes insecure or depressed. It's as if recognition is fuel; the absence of it brings an energetic engagement with the world to a dead stop. Worse, such frustration causes a person to feel that the need for recognition is itself a bad thing, as if he or she shouldn't need to be recognized.

<u>Everyone needs it, but few get it</u>

It is a universal feature of childhood that when a need is frustrated, the frustration comes to feel normal and the need itself problematic. As a result, the person not only can't get enough recognition, but can't easily give it to others.

And yet, recognition is a vital nutrient for psychological growth and health. Think of the reaction of a baby when you make eye contact—one mother told me she felt that the baby had been plugged into an electric socket. Just being *seen* is enough to energize a baby. We praise children for what they do, for the challenges they succeed in mastering. We put their scribbles on our refrigerator doors as if they're masterpieces. Some people do this instinctively; no one has to tell them that it is important for their kids' growth and development or that it builds their self-esteem. For others, such intuitions are blocked or missing, and their children suffer. There is evidence, however, that the bare but vital bones of recognition can be taught and learned, whether by parents or, more germane for our purposes, progressive leaders.

When those children grow up and become the leaders of progressive organizations, many think that they—and others—don't or shouldn't need this kind of attention anymore, as if the need for affirmation disappears at high school graduation. That's why we so often hear leaders say things like, "We don't baby our people here." Babies need recognition; adults, apparently, only need a paycheck. Not only is there a library of studies that demonstrate the opposite, but, in their hearts, the leaders uttering a "tough love" approach to learning and development know it too. Their problem is that they begrudge, fear, and even feel guilty about taking seriously what they already know. They begrudge it because they didn't get it when *they* were coming up. They fear having to face the degree to which they, themselves, need recognition. And they feel guilty about how much they want it.

It's hard to give what you never got.

But what do progressive leaders feel guilty about? Perhaps the answer can be found in the oft-heard cliché, "we're working for our members," or for "the people," or for the "preservation of the Earth, itself." The problem isn't that the content of such comments is wrong, but that it too often expresses organizers' and leaders' need to be martyrs, justifying their own self-denial and deprivation of recognition on the grounds that their job is to give, not get; to take care of others, not themselves.

In my practice as a psychotherapist, I've seen dozens of people who grew up in environments in which nothing they did was recognized and praised, or only Herculean accomplishments were noticed. One patient told me that she was expected to bring home A's but rarely got as much as a pat on the back for them. Another told me that, with five siblings, it was unusual for his mother to notice if he even *went* to school, much less excelled there. Another patient had a father who always one-upped his son's accomplishments, as if the son's gain was the father's loss. And still another patient was, as a child, her mother's nursemaid through prolonged illnesses, yet when the patient needed her mother's help, her mother criticized her for being a burden. In all these cases, the children grew up insecure about whether they were competent and lovable.

These patterns persist long after childhood. The leaders uttering a "tough love" approach to learning and development might be these children grown up. Like my patients, they were starved. And when a person is actually starved, the stomach shrinks. In fact, the deprivations families inflict are rarely even acknowledged as injuries because they just feel like a normal part of growing up.

Recognition is about specialness

Most people can remember at least one teacher from their past who had a deep and meaningful impact by virtue of recognizing something special about them. The recognition might have come in the form of praise or extra time, or the imposition of high standards; the common denominator is that the student felt special and recognized.

An older psychiatrist once told me that, in his 50 years of treating couples, the one predictor of marital success was the ability of each person in the couple to love the ways that the other person was *different*. Happiness was all about recognition.

To be recognized is to be known and appreciated for what makes you unique. Employees often joke that lots of generic praise from an employer is proof that the employer doesn't really care. The jokes are appropriate—generic praise is usually empty praise. And praising an individual for generic accomplishments is similarly empty. Acknowledgments of specific actions in concrete ways, on the other hand, are powerful. For recognition to have maximum value, it should be frequent, specific, timely, and attuned to the particularity of the person.

Another essential dimension of recognition is the communication that another person is important. The content might involve something specific, but the underlying message is, "You are important enough for me to notice what you're doing and valuable enough to me to make it worth my time telling you about it." That's why, in children, recognition builds self-esteem and why its absence leads to suffering. Without recognition, children feel they don't matter, that they're invisible. They may try to get recognition in negative ways. They may stop trying altogether.

Adults do the same thing. In the absence of recognition, they feel that their work, their abilities, their very selves have little value. They lose any sense of excitement or passion. They may start to feel like cogs in a machine, rather than a vital part of a team, and eventually give up altogether.

If recognition involves being seen for our authentic selves, for having some special value, then racism might represent the ultimate in mis- or nonrecognition. One of the hallmarks of racial prejudice is the assumption that rewards and punishments are distributed on the basis of whether an individual belongs to a certain class of people. Prerogatives are conferred without any regard for individual value or competence or qualification. The person of color is still often systematically *not recognized* as deserving. The individual disappears behind the generic mask of race.

Similarly, not only are women in the workforce paid less than men, but hardly a week goes by that I don't hear a woman recount a situation in which her voice was drowned out or ignored by a man or men. She felt invisible. Her ideas were appropriated by a man who then claimed—and was given—credit. This is the sine qua non of nonrecognition.

Progressives suffer from a lack of recognition

In my many years of teaching progressive leaders, I've had occasion to give dozens of talks and trainings. The one that regularly evoked the strongest emotion by far was one that focused on the importance of recognition. Some people, including the most hardheaded leaders, routinely teared up when asked to reflect on the presence or absence of recognition in their workplaces. Stories about working hard and putting in countless hours that were never acknowledged were commonplace.

I told them that they were like camels, adapted to go for long distances without water—in this case, without recognition. Universally, people agreed and either laughed or cried about it. I told them they were starving for recognition, but that they had come to believe it was nowhere to be found when, in fact, it was all around them. I would give them homework: Make a point of providing some realistic and appropriate recognition to someone they worked with every day. They came back with stories of how moved and appreciative the other person was. One recipient of praise said, "I've been in the labor movement for 30 years and this is the first time anyone has ever asked about me." Such a small investment; such a huge return.

One leader reported that he had decided to visit the back office and accounting division of his large organization and just hang out with the clerical staff. He spent 15 minutes there, doing little else but spending time in friendly conversation. To his surprise, the staff talked about his visit all day and was markedly more animated in their work. In this case, the recognition he offered didn't come in the form of praise, but simply in his presence. All he did was sit, listen, make small talk, and joke around. But that wasn't what was really going on. What was really going on was that he was conferring a dose of powerful recognition on these back-office staff; powerful because the underlying authority relationship shaped the meaning of the interaction. It takes very little for someone to feel special in relationship to an esteemed leader. Since the leader's time is implicitly understood as valuable, his or her very attention communicates that the subordinate is valuable and worthwhile.

Some progressive leaders appear surprised that their followers feel this way, that they want to have their picture taken with their president or CEO. The best leaders understand this dynamic and use it generously and strategically, incorporating it into their strategies for influencing their organizations and constituencies. They intuitively understand what psychologists call *transference*—the near-universal phenomenon in which people project onto relationships with authorities the feelings they had toward the authorities of childhood—their all-important caretakers.

Leaders who understand transference don't have to know it by name, but they instinctively make use of it every single day. Great politicians are the consummate practitioners of this art form. At a recent fundraiser in San Francisco, a ticket to attend and listen to a very prominent politician cost $1,000. For $2,000, you could also have your picture taken with him.

Attention and recognition are powerful reward systems

If a leader's attention is especially valuable to a staff member or constituent, then a valuable opportunity is lost when leaders don't feel comfortable using recognition in a strategic and political way. The culture of an organization is importantly shaped by who gets positive attention and what kinds of work get rewarded. If you want your staff and members to mentor other people, take on more responsibility, be more accountable, or take more risks, then one of the most powerful reward systems available to you is the attention and validation you offer to reinforce such behavior. And yet, time after time, we have talked to progressive leaders too uncomfortable with their own interpersonal influence to use it to shape the direction of their organizations.

Equally interesting in our work with progressive leaders was the ironic—but universal—finding that most leaders and organizers felt that they themselves were very good at giving recognition while simultaneously complaining about the dearth of it when it came to receiving it. The irony was obvious: If everyone says they're good at *giving* recognition but never get it, something doesn't compute. The answer is that they're not really good at giving recognition at all, that their view of themselves as generous in this regard is completely distorted and leads them regularly to view crumbs of recognition as a whole loaf. Almost no one we worked with was especially good at providing the whole loaf. Instead, everyone contributed to creating the desert in which starvation was considered normal.

Don't always do unto others as was done unto you

An organizational culture in which people don't feel seen or appreciated usually has a story about why such practices (or the lack thereof) are normal or healthy. But when you get beneath the rationalizations, you begin to hear the truth: People do unto others as was done unto them. I was talking with a leader of a union who was engaged in tough bargaining with an employer. He was waxing eloquent about his approach to developing young organizers being trained to do bargaining. He said, "I let them watch me a few times and then I just throw them into the deep end and tell them to swim. I don't believe in holding their hands or coddling them." I asked him, "Well, what about someone who is talented but might—for his or her own individual reasons—*need* a lot of hand-holding; what do you do then?" For a moment, he seemed stumped, as if he didn't quite understand my question. "Well, I do it my way anyway," he said. "If they wash out, they wash out." And then he added the crucial fact: "That's the way it was done with me."

In fact, this fellow had a rigid, strict, and somewhat harsh temperament. He was doing what psychologists call "turning passive into active," or "identifying with the aggressor." His behavior reminds me of an early scene in the 1977 film "Saturday Night Fever": The working-class Manero family is sitting around the dinner table. The mother, frustrated at her husband's loss of his job, smacks him upside his head. The father then does the same to his son, Tony (played by John Travolta), who passes along the smack to his younger sister. When we endure and then survive and master hardships, we tend to drift toward becoming the creator of hardship rather than its victim. And then we normalize it; we make a virtue out of a necessity.

The bottom line: It's difficult to give to others what was not given to us. But mature leaders are those who transcend their own childhood experiences out of service to the organization.

It's OK to want some yourself

Social movements are based on the understanding that whether in democracies or totalitarian states, leaders do nothing if they are not pressured into action by ordinary people. Unions are founded on the truth that it is working people, not bosses, who create the value that produces profit and prosperity. At a strike meeting in San Francisco, I recently had occasion to hear a leader of a hotel workers union speaking to members. "[The hotel owners] treat you like dirt, but the fact is that they need you," he said. "You—not they—are the backbone of San Francisco's hotel industry. And the hotels are the backbone of San Francisco's hospitality industry, an industry essential to the city's economic health. Without you, San Francisco would be Fresno" (a much smaller, somewhat depressed and unsophisticated city in the Central Valley of California)!

It was hardly an unusual exhortation to action. You can probably hear hundreds of versions of the same inspiring idea being voiced in workplaces and union halls any day of the week anywhere in the world.

Yet inside their own walls, progressive organizations seem to have a special resistance to moving past cultures of stingy recognition. The problem is guilt: Telling themselves that they're driven by a mission—not by selfish needs for material or personal rewards—progressive lead-ers and organizers tend to feel guilty about indulging their own needs, feeling they should subordinate those needs to the needs of the constituencies they're serving.

One group I worked with proudly told me that, after de-cades of a principled refusal to single out anyone on their staff for special commendations, they had finally solved this problem. They had recently agreed to award some-one who had led a major campaign a small, inexpensive pin at a modest victory dinner. Since I had become quite friendly with this group and had earned their trust, I felt I could poke and provoke them. I said, in a serious voice: "Hmm. OK. Your major breakthrough in affording each other recognition involves one small pin for one person. One time? You know, you guys remind me of a family that's been isolated from all human contact on a deserted island for generations and has developed these bizarre ideas. Then all of a sudden some anthropologist discovers them and is stunned by how completely dysfunctional and crazy they've become!" There was a pause and then the room erupted into gales of laughter as they recognized—for the first time—something strange and symptomatic about them that had seemed completely normal.

In a telling follow-up session to this meeting, I led an "appreciation exercise" in which each person on the team was to stand up at a flip chart, his or her back to the group, and write down the comments that each person on the team made about what was especially valuable about the person standing at the easel. Amid a fair amount of good-natured (and embarrassed) joking, the exercise generated honest and highly personal feedback. The outcome was poignant—the looks on people's faces as they took in the appreciation of their colleagues. A few cried. Others became still and reflective. And still others openly acknowledged that they had never before heard anyone say these things to them; the experience was deeply moving.

So, recognition can be conferred in many different ways. It can be praise or simply attention. It can be giving someone feedback, not all of it even good, or it can be the grand theatrics of an awards ceremony. It can be a note indicating that someone important to you is thinking about you, or it can be singling you out. The crucial dimension of the experience, however, is that the person feels that the recognition is *specific* to him or her, that it's particular, that it recognizes something special and unique.

For leaders of progressive organizations, the opportunities to provide recognition are everywhere, and yet we're blind to them. When people are given meaningful roles, they feel recognized. When they are genuinely asked for their opinions, they feel recognized. When they're respectfully held accountable, they feel recognized. When we would start retreats by asking people to tell their story, they would feel recognized. One person said to me, "Just the fact that we're taking time in a conference for me to talk to someone about who I am totally breaks the mold of our organization."

The history of the black church, the foundational platform upon which the civil rights movement grew, is perhaps the most dramatic history of a recognition-based culture. Church structure consisted of standing committees and work groups—highly organized, structured, task-oriented, and coordinated. In addition, there were frequent and highly organized social activities that engaged large numbers of people. Participation in church life was extremely high, regardless of age or gender. Roles proliferated and were recognized as important. Members were made to feel important, an experience denied them in the larger society.

Even small expressions of appreciation matter

I used to be embarrassed when I would walk through a hospital or agency and see pictures of employees on the wall with "employee of the month" plaques underneath. I cynically pictured the employee saying something like, "That's great that you hand out a plaque, but a raise would have been a lot nicer!" Imagine my vexation when I began to read about companies that did nothing else but help other companies develop systems of recognition for the latters' employees. I'm not talking about compensation consultants, but *recognition consultants* who help managers and supervisors design special Post-it notes to deliver feedback and praise, or special gifts, rituals, and complicated hierarchies of social events to do the same. My first impulse was, again—"Oh no—there's no way that little tchotchkes and a 'lunch-with-the-boss' is going to fool employees into being happy and productive!"

Of course, it was I who was the fool. The rewards were symbolic, but gestures such as these, if made authentically, have profound effects on employees because they speak to a basic human need. A groundbreaking study of 200,000 employees in the private sector conducted by the Jackson Organization and reported several years ago by Adam Gostick and Chester Elton persuasively demonstrated a direct link between employee recognition and multiple financial indicators. Return on equity and return on assets were three times higher in organizations with effective ways of recognizing employee excellence. In addition, when asked to rate managers on a scale labeled "Does a good job of recognizing employee contributions," those teams with highly rated managers also got the top scores for customer satisfaction. Finally, employees who felt recognized demonstrated greater innovation and creativity, took more personal responsibility, demonstrated a greater desire to contribute to the success of the company, and had a stronger emotional bond to the organization and its goals. The conclusion of the study is one that progressive organizations should duly note: *People work harder at places where they feel recognized and valued for their unique contributions. And valued and engaged employees bring great value and profit to their organizations.*

An article in the Harvard Business Review by Edward Hallowell, M.D., debunks the time-honored axiom that people usually "learn from their mistakes." In fact, Hallowell shows that most people feel embarrassed or upset when they make mistakes and try to forget or cover up what happened. Hallowell describes a study done at MIT that showed that monkeys who were successful performing a task did even better on the next one, while those who failed showed no improvement.

Hallowell also describes a moving ceremony at Harvard called "Harvard Heroes" that sought to honor non-academic employees. One such employee, an older man named Manny Diogenes, had worked for 27 years as a caretaker for one of the freshman houses. He didn't miss a single day of work. Harvard's president, the master of ceremonies for this event, read a letter from a freshman who said that Manny had, in effect, substituted for his family during times of intense and painful homesickness. The president turned and pointed at Manny and bellowed: "Manny Diogenes, I pronounce *you* to be a Harvard hero!"

Tears streamed down Manny's face, as well as the faces of his family and half the audience. At that moment, it was hard not to believe that such public recognition wasn't at least as important to Manny as a bigger paycheck.

The types of recognition that had the greatest effect on employees were those that linked the individual's contribution to the team, to the productivity of the whole. The individual's efforts were recognized as unique but were framed within a context of the values and purpose of the group. In other words, such recognition simultaneously spoke to the need for both recognition *and* meaning.

Even seemingly cynical expressions of recognition have a positive effect. In every major city in the country—and especially in Washington, D.C.—every night, dozens of "leaders" are being officially recognized. The honoree, and everyone attending these events, knows that the purpose of this "recognition" is probably to directly or indirectly raise money. The more important the person being honored, the more money you can shake out of that person's contacts, associates, vendors, and friends. Everyone knows that it is a money game. In spite of knowing the game and their role as pawns in it, most of those being "recognized" still love it. For a few minutes, such a person—for example, a politician—thinks, "I'm not just one of 535 members of Congress. I am not just another leader or funder of an organization. I stand out above the crowd."

But you don't need plaques or ceremonies to let people know they are unique and uniquely valued. Five years ago, my father died, and a leader I greatly admired wrote me a short condolence note, including in it something very specific about my father. It didn't matter to me one bit that a friend of mine had supplied that leader with this information. I was touched and grateful, and my willingness to work for this man increased.

The crucial characteristics of genuine and effective recognition is that it is *specific* and *personal*—particular to one person, and acknowledging something special and unique about that person.

Recognition is as valuable as money

The jury is no longer out about the relative importance of recognition and money. Both are crucial. Organizations that provide little recognition *have* to pay employees a lot of money. Those that provide an environment that is rich in recognition, meaning, and purpose can often ask for financial sacrifices. Progressive organizations that can't reward staff and members with financial incentives have a special obligation to create systems of recognition that are embedded in the everyday practices and culture of their organizations. William James once said, "What every genuine philosopher (every genuine man, in fact) craves most is praise—although the philosophers generally call it 'recognition!'" Whatever you call it, in this crucial way, we are all philosophers.

Summary

1) Recognition is a vital nutrient for psychological growth and health. But so many people fail to get enough of it as children that they have a hard time passing it on.

2) Recognition is about specialness. Generic praise doesn't cut it. People need to be acknowledged for what is unique about them—and that means knowing who they are.

3) Progressive organizers and leaders are starved for recognition but have adapted to its absence because of a self-sabotaging belief that they don't deserve it. After all, they are merely serving others who are less fortunate. Mission-driven work is supposed to be its own reward.

4) Recognition can be provided in small acts or expressions of appreciation (provided they are not generic), but also through giving people real roles to perform that are important and for which they are held accountable.

CHAPTER SIX

The Need for Agency

Definition: The need to have a "voice," to learn, to be creative, and to be able to influence one's environment

[Humans'] capacity to intervene, to compare, to judge, to decide, to choose, to desist makes them capable of acts of greatness and of dignity.

—Paulo Freire, philosopher and educator

Consider the following experiment: A mother is asked to be completely expressionless—to have a "still face"—in response to her baby's attempts to communicate. Initially, the infant responds with an increased effort to connect, but then becomes agitated, disorganized, and eventually withdraws.

The experiment demonstrates the importance of what psychologists call "contingency," the experience of the world (in this case, the mother) responding accurately and appropriately to our actions and needs. If the human environment is immune to the child's gestures and communications, or responds in a way that negates the child's intentions, then the child comes to feel weak, unimportant, and devalued.

But if the environment provides enough contingent responses, then the child's sense of self is strengthened; he or she becomes more vital and alive, and begins to feel a growing sense of efficacy in the world. The child grows up learning that his or her intentions, desires, gestures, and feelings *matter*, that the world is not only attuned, but that the child can elicit and influence that attunement.

We learn and take risks only if we can influence our world

When a child's need for contingent responses is reasonably met, he or she can also take risks. Child development experts devised an experiment called "the visual cliff" to demonstrate this finding. A table is covered by a piece of clear glass long enough to extend two feet over one end. A six-month-old baby is put on the table and encouraged by his or her mother to crawl to the end of it. The baby's eyes tell him or her that the table ends, and that to continue, therefore, is to fall off the "cliff." However, the baby's tactile senses suggest that it's safe. The baby wants to reach its mother and is also fearful.

What determines whether the baby has the confidence to risk continuing? The researchers found that it was the response of the environment, i.e., the mother. If the baby's mother stands at the end of the glass, happily and confidently encouraging the baby to risk it, he or she will risk it. The mother's enthusiastic invitation directly mirrors and is responsive to the baby's wish to explore. If, on the other hand, the mother looks worried or isn't paying attention, the baby stops and refuses to advance.

The experience of contingency, or the lack thereof, continues throughout life. Siblings, peers, teachers, employers, and political institutions are all potential grantors or deniers of contingency, of either responsiveness or the rejection inherent in the "still face." When someone feels that his or her voice matters, that he or she "counts"—that, to quote Jesse Jackson, he or she is "somebody"—then it's safe to learn and be creative.

On the other hand, if the world has a constant "still face," or otherwise thwarts the person's desires and intentions, then she or he ultimately gives up and dampens whatever passion, curiosity, and liveliness was there. Exercising creativity depends on the implicit belief that we have the right to express ourselves, to let loose with pleasure the imaginative and playful capacity and yearnings of our minds in ways that are recognized by the world.

Just like the risk the baby takes in the visual cliff experiment when its mother is close by and encouraging, optimal learning depends on safe nurturing mentors and environments. Progressive educators regularly argue that the empathic relationship between teacher and student is a better predictor of academic outcome than all the metrics and market-based criteria that business and government can come up with. David Kirp, professor of public policy at the Goldman School of Public Policy at the University of California, Berkeley, argued in a recent New York Times editorial that, "Every successful educational initiative of which I'm aware aims at strengthening personal bonds by building strong systems of support in the schools," According to his research, "The best preschools create intimate worlds where students become explorers and attentive adults are close at hand."

Everybody needs to "be somebody"

The experience of exerting influence or control over our environment, as well as the right to express creativity and the confidence to take risks, are all part of human *agency*. Agency is a basic need, every bit as important as the need for economic security and justice. Agency animates us in every area of our lives. It is connected to lofty ideals like self-determination, autonomy, and freedom. It's what is meant when a teacher tells a student, "I want to hear more of *your voice* in this essay," or when a political movement argues that women or people of color need a *voice* in decision-making.

The feeling that we have a "voice" or not can be literal. An acting coach recently said to me, "It's amazing to me how many people I work with who genuinely don't feel like they have the right to speak, so much so that their voices become small, strangled. They are afraid to make bold interpretations with the text for fear of getting it wrong."

The positive effects of agency have been demonstrated in studies of the brain. In a series of groundbreaking studies in the '60s and '70s, neuroscientists showed that when laboratory rats have a chance to learn and influence their environment (e.g., by having control over food or the cessation of noxious stimuli), their brain cells grow and establish new connections much faster than those of animals that lack these opportunities. Under the microscope, the brains of the contingent learners look like a dense redwood forest; those not able to learn, in deprived environments over which they had little control, have brains that look like a stand of bare trees in the dead of winter.

As such, progressive organizations seeking maximum growth, passion, and flexibility must ensure that both within their staff culture and in their external organizing, the need for agency is addressed and gratified. In some ways, labor unions and other community organizations built to exercise power intuitively understand this. Agency, and its opposite—helplessness—have long been in the cross hairs of political organizations that represent the underdog. The relevance of power and opportunity for self-esteem and passion wouldn't be a news flash to any of these organizations. However, it did take the field of psychology a while to catch up with what organizers since Moses, Mother Jones, John L. Lewis, and Saul Alinsky knew for a long time.

Learned helplessness

In 1965, Martin Seligman and Steven Maier, young psychology graduate students at the University of Pennsylvania, did an experiment that changed the way psychologists think about agency. Their special contribution was in linking it to a social, or relational, theory about depression. Seligman and Maier taught one dog that it could escape a mild electric shock by pressing a lever. At the same moment, in another cage, a second dog got the exact same electric shock—it was, in effect, "yoked" to that of the first dog—but nothing the second dog did would stop the shock. When the first dog pressed the lever, the shocks applied to *both dogs* ceased. The first dog learned that it could take an action to control its environment, while the second dog learned that nothing it did would change anything.

Seligman and Maier then placed each dog in something called a "shuttlebox," a large rectangular box with two compartments separated only by a very low wall. When the first dog—the one that learned it had agency—was placed in one compartment of the shuttlebox and given an electric shock that could easily be escaped by hopping over the fence into the other compartment, that's exactly what it did. In the same circumstances—same box, same wall, same shock—the dog that had learned it was helpless lay down and passively endured it. Seligman and Maier concluded that they had experimentally induced the equivalent of depression in the second dog and that it stemmed from its experience of helplessness. Seligman and Maier called this "learned helplessness."

Learned helplessness explains one way that, even absent biological factors, people can become depressed and passive. This concept also explains a lot about politics and political apathy. Powerlessness breeds passivity.

Institutions benefit when members have agency

When individuals are given opportunities to learn, take responsibility, and make decisions, the institutions they're associated with also benefit. At a megachurch we visited a few years ago, we were met in the parking lot by a "greeter," handed off to someone else who gave us a tour, and served coffee by another volunteer, all before we met anyone connected to the paid ministry of the church. When an institution gives people real roles with real responsibility, roles aligned with their personal interests, their need for agency is met, along with needs for community and meaning. This is good for the institution, too, which gains an engaged, loyal adherent.

In the New York Times Op-Ed about education mentioned earlier, David Kirp cites Harvard Business School historian and Pulitzer Prize winner Alfred D. Chandler Jr., who demonstrated that businesses prospered by developing "organizational capabilities," putting effective systems in place and *encouraging learning inside the organization.*

Progressive organizations seeking maximum growth, passion, and flexibility must ensure that the need for agency is addressed and gratified both within their staff culture and in their external organizing. Labor unions and other community organizations built to exercise power intuitively understand this. Unions were formed to redress both the economic and psychic costs of the powerlessness of workers. Unable to influence—much less control—the conditions of their employment or the process of production, workers were subject to gross economic exploitation and the arbitrary power of their bosses in every area of their lives. There was no lever to press to stop the shocks, no wall to step over to secure greater security and well-being. Unions were the original—and continue to be the only—curb on the employer's power in the workplace, the only reliable lever that workers possess to exercise control over their working conditions, to influence the process and outcome of their labor.

Every organizer, union or nonunion, with whom we've worked understands this. In fact, a frequent organizing technique is for an organizer to take a group of workers or community members with him or her and deliberately pick a fight with an especially intimidating boss, politician, or agency, precisely to demonstrate that, through collective action, people aren't dogs in cages but human beings worthy of respect, dignity, and a measure of self-determination. Often the fiercest political battles don't involve money or benefits, but the rights of people to exercise some control over their working conditions and the institutions that serve their communities.

People in power also recognize this. A top negotiator for the owners of a nursing home chain once told me that her view of bargaining with nurses in her company was simple: "Giving them money is easy, but we can't let them have a say in staffing ratios because we need that flexibility to maximize our profits." The employer would much rather give workers money than too much agency. Too often, union leaders have felt forced to take the money.

When Japanese cars were gobbling up an increasing share of the American market in the '70s and '80s, U.S. business strategists and organizational psychologists began to study the Japanese factory system. These studies clearly revealed that one competitive advantage of Japanese production systems was the engagement of workers—the satisfaction of their needs for agency, relationships, and meaning. Teamwork, participation in a companywide "community," and an identification with their company's wider social role all seemed to compensate for some of the hardship of the assembly line, thereby mitigating worker demands for higher wages.

For example, American researchers noticed a custom in Japanese factories in which any individual worker who spots a defect could shut down the entire line simply by pulling a thin nylon strip called the "Andon cord," and do so without the authorization of a higher-up. American auto company managers were, however, afraid that workers would abuse this opportunity for agency. Their experience was the opposite—workers appreciated the trust placed in them. Peers kept them from acting destructively. The lesson: Agency doesn't mean omnipotence. Recognizing the agency of others doesn't mean giving over control to them. It means recognizing that people need to shape their world and be more self-determining. In fact, the more you provide an environment that encourages agency, the more you can also emphasize accountability.

Organizations that offer opportunities for learning reap rewards beyond the increased expertise or knowledge the learners offer. We once offered several progressive organizations the opportunity for their members to learn "digital storytelling," a process of putting together short, first-person video and PowerPoint narratives about their lives and their involvement with politics by combining recorded voice, still and moving images, and music or other sounds. By all accounts, the experience was extremely meaningful to its participants. They learned that they had talent; they could master technologies they thought were beyond them, and create something that moved others. And these accomplishments won them the recognition of their peers. Equally important, they expressed gratitude to their organization for the chance to experience such success. They became more engaged.

Even people who have lost considerable ability to take care of themselves and the daily tasks of living continue to need to exercise agency. Extensive research has been done in nursing homes on the effects of giving residents greater control over such things as décor, social activities, and meal choices. The results of one study were striking: Compared with a similar group who didn't have such choices, the residents who did have such power initiated more social interactions and described themselves as happier. Most startling: After 18 months, the death rate in the "agency" group was half that of the other group. In study after study, nursing home residents rank autonomy as more important to their quality of life than meals or bathing.

Thwarted agency breeds complainers and consumers

People who are deprived of healthy agency are likely to express agency in destructive ways. If people can't exercise self-determination by saying yes to the life they want to lead, they will more than likely exercise the power to say no. If they can't shape the direction of events around them, they unconsciously try to obstruct them. The analogy might be a toddler who is, in fact, helpless in shaping his or her daily life but can wreak havoc on his parents' ability to shape it.

At the workplace, people's frustration takes the form of carping and being demanding. Again, the logic is not hard to understand: If they can't have real control, they'll try to control the process from below by being critical and acting entitled. If people aren't treated like active agents capable of making important decisions, then they won't "follow" leaders anywhere unless their narrowest self-interest—money—is satisfied.

Empowerment such as this explains findings reported in an op-ed by John Guida in the New York Times on January 13, 2015 that belonging to a union brings greater life satisfaction for reasons quite different than the benefits derived from higher wages and retirement security; namely, an increased sense of participation, connectedness, and agency.

In public life, if people view government as beyond their influence and politicians as "still faces" unresponsive to their needs and desires, their repressed needs for agency sometimes erupt in extreme forms of anti-government paranoia. Further, many social theorists argue that Americans' unmet needs for agency are behind our seemingly unquenchable thirst for consumption. The freedom to shop may feel like the last domain of agency.

We confer agency by giving people real roles

If you don't want the people you serve or organize to become complainers or act like victims, you have to offer them agency. And one of the most powerful ways that a progressive organization can do that is to give people real roles in the organization. If the role is window-dressing or the expectation is simply that someone show up, then little more than that can be expected. But if staff and leaders commit themselves to getting to know their members as people with lives, passions, and concerns outside their workplaces, they will almost certainly discover talents and interests that can be meaningfully molded into roles that help the union in its campaigns.

One group we visited was composed mostly of immigrants. Upon engaging them in deeper conversations, we found that their backgrounds were highly varied and often included extraordinary—but untapped—skills. One had been a judge in his home country, another a successful painter, another had counseled gang leaders, and still another had been an academic who had published extensively about unions! It was easy to see how these skills and experiences could be shaped into roles that meaningfully deployed the agency and creativity of these workers and served the organization's greater purposes in the process.

To create new leaders, leaders must feel their own agency

I've worked with leaders of the progressive movement for decades, and it is striking how often I encounter what may be a hidden impediment to their ability to nurture a sense of agency in staff, members, or constituents. That obstacle is the unspoken conviction of the leaders themselves that they are frauds, imposters; that they don't deserve to be in the positions they hold, and that if they aren't vigilant, they will be found out, rejected, and humiliated. Their childhoods were often marked by a conviction that they were not really supposed to have more of the good things in life than their families or communities; that they weren't supposed to be more successful, powerful, or admired than their caretakers and peers.

They may have achieved a lot in spite of this belief, but then couldn't really embrace their success or feel fully deserving of it. That meant they couldn't exercise the power—the agency—that went with their achievement with a relaxed and confident sense of entitlement. This led them to be martyrs, perfectionists, strategically conservative, or chronically anxious and self-defeating. They became cynical, resigned to the status quo. The problematic heart of the matter was a belief that being an important leader in something inspiring, ambitious, and grand put them at risk of exposure and humiliation.

If leaders cannot own their right to agency, how can they recognize the talents and abilities of those around them? How can they encourage others to speak up and rise up, to take control and use power? How can they envision those around them as anything other than the "masses" or the "rank and file"—people who should "know their place?"

A movement of leaders can be ours

We need to step away from images of "the masses," or the "rank and file" to a movement that sees itself as a collection of thousands of leaders—people who initiate, connect, call meetings, reflect together, and take others into action. Our movement cannot have too many leaders. But to have the leaders we need, we have to break apart our old understandings of thinkers and doers, leaders and followers, those on top and those on the bottom, and recruit and develop the talent that surrounds us. Any organization that aims to develop its members and staff as leaders who take risks, innovate, hold themselves accountable, are motivated to nurture other, equally responsible and creative leaders—and are in it for the long run—must provide enormous space for people to act on their profound human need for agency.

There is nothing wrong with "the people." They will step up to increasing roles and responsibilities if we treat them like the complex human beings they are.

<u>Summary</u>

1) If the human environment is immune to the child's gestures and communications, or responds in a way that negates the child's intentions, then the child comes to feel weak, unimportant, and devalued.

2) When someone feels his or her voice matters, that he or she "counts," then it's safe to learn and be creative.

3) When people can't influence their environments, they feel helpless, passive, and are likely to become complaining consumers.

4) When people are given real roles in an organization or movement, they gain a sense of agency, and are much more likely to become engaged in the mission of that organization and movement.

5) Our movement cannot have too many leaders.

6) People will regularly sacrifice economic rewards for the satisfactions inherent in empowerment and agency.

CONCLUSION

"You are not here merely to make a living. You are here in order to enable the world to live more amply, with greater vision, with a finer spirit of hope and achievement. You are here to enrich the world, and you impoverish yourself if you forget the errand."

—President Woodrow Wilson

Attacks from the Right have been relentless, well-funded, and aimed at the core of the progressive agenda. It's not hard to fathom why the Left's organizations seem to demand constant toil and "business as usual." I have no trouble understanding why progressive organizers might want to dismiss a plea like this one to reflect more deeply on issues of human nature.

Yet I believe that the future of our movement depends on such reflection. Because despite tremendous efforts, our side is slowly but steadily losing. Finding ways to embed a more accurate and comprehensive view of what makes people tick in our leadership styles, organizational practices, culture, and agendas is a necessary part of building power through creating healthier institutions.

Throughout history, the most important political victories of liberals and radicals have been shot through with appeals to needs other than narrow economic ones. The spirit of the women's suffrage movement was grounded in demands for empowerment, respect, and equality. The early appearance of labor unions resonated not only with demands for economic justice but with the need for solidarity. The government programs passed under the auspices of the New Deal were economic in nature, but the popular consensus that gave Roosevelt the leverage to pass them came from feelings of empathy in hardship and collective purpose in pulling through the Depression.

The civil rights movement succeeded because of a growing consciousness that demeaning people on the basis of race violated both spiritual calls for fairness and basic American values. The environmental movement may advocate for a carbon tax, but to the extent it is successful, it is because it elicits a love for the Earth, for something greater than the self. And, finally, candidate Barack Obama did not win the 2008 election on the strength of the details of his economic policies. He called Americans to a higher purpose and stimulated our need for meaning—and Americans responded.

This book is primarily about what people need, not specifically about how to give it to them. It argues that people vote, turn out for demonstrations, and actively engage with organizations that speak to them as feeling—not just thinking—beings, that economic survival and justice are only two needs, equal to and even sometimes surpassed by needs for meaning, recognition, relationship, and agency.

That said, I've offered some concrete suggestions and examples—drawn from our work at the Institute4Change—of how organizations can incorporate a broader view of human needs. Future publications from those involved with the Institute4Change will elaborate these suggestions at much greater length.

Leaders and organizers need to become more self-reflective about their own needs, thus undermining an ethic of unhealthy physical and psychological self-care. Organizations can offer bolder visions that inspire and stimulate needs for meaning and purpose rather than simply focus on electoral victories. Organizers can bring curiosity, active listening, and some degree of self-disclosure to conversations and group meetings, thus speaking to people's need for relationship and recognition. A similar outcome can be facilitated by giving people real roles—with appropriate feedback—and holding them accountable. Leaders can become learners. They can allow staff, members, and participants at all levels greater opportunities to increase their knowledge and skills, be creative, and affect the organization in ways that promote feelings of agency.

We hope this book inspires progressives to look more deeply into themselves and their practices, not just for its own sake but to help progressive activists and leaders create a broader and firmer institutional base for a social change movement. Satisfying a wide range of human needs is not just the means to an end, it *is* the end. The movement we envision achieves not just economic justice, decent wages, good health care, or affordable education, it creates a world in which everyone's life is rich in purpose and belonging, meaning, and happiness.

ACKNOWLEDGMENTS

In 2002, a small group of practitioners drawn from the highest levels of the worlds of political and community organizing, psychology, organizational change, and business strategy came together to start an organization that eventually became the Institute4Change. Our aim was to work with progressive organizations and groups to help them become bolder, healthier, and more strategic, all as a means of increasing their political power. We soon also recruited actors to our faculty in the belief that leaders needed help with their public personas, how they carried themselves and spoke in public, and, therefore, how they could tell their "story" in more effective ways. Our belief was, from the beginning, that the most effective approach to stimulating the radical changes that both we and the leaders who hired us envisioned required expertise drawn from many different sources, from a "multitude of voices."

Thus, the ideas in this book, to the extent that they were drawn from my 12 years of experience with the Institute4Change, grew in a rich multidisciplinary soup of highly varied perspectives. For that reason, at some points I use the pronoun "I" and at other times, "we." The one thing all of us had in common was the awareness that our own individual expertise was but one color in a large palette and that we needed to learn from each other in order to be effective.

My teammates taught me an enormous amount that eventually found its way into this book. I want to give special thanks to: Michael McGrath, a 25-year veteran practitioner, teacher, and writer in the areas of executive and organizational development and talent management, currently on the faculty of the University of Michigan; Anthony Miles, formerly a senior partner and managing director of the Boston Consulting Group; George Gates, an organizational development consultant with over 30 years' experience, much of it focused specifically on improving labor/management relationships; Ken Smith, formerly a lead organizer for the Industrial Areas Foundation, originally founded by Saul Alinsky; Tom De Bruin, from the Service Employees International Union, one of the best organizers and leaders in the American labor movement over the last 20 years; Brian Lohmann, actor, coach, and improvisation instructor; and Robert Kegan and Lisa Lahey, Harvard professors who developed a unique approach to helping large numbers of individuals make profound psychological changes.

However, the person from whom I have learned the most has been Larry McNeil, formerly the West Coast director of the Industrial Areas Foundation, and founder and executive director of the Institute4Change. Larry's influence on my own thinking about what progressive leaders and organizations need today in order to change and become more powerful has been so profound that there are many points in this book that reflect his thinking more than my own. He taught me about organizing, about how to analyze power, and about what makes for a healthy and vibrant political organization. He tutored me about the nature of leadership, vision, and, most of all, about how all of our theories, teaching, and consulting had to help our clients *win*. Although an intellectual himself, Larry's approach to political and organizational change mirrored my own approach to psychotherapy; namely, that the only things that matter in the end are outcomes.

I was originally inspired to think about the political implications of the need for meaning by my friends and colleagues, Michael Lerner and Peter Gabel.

In my own field of psychology, insights derived from psychoanalysis inform this book, especially those developed by psychoanalyst and researcher Joseph Weiss, M.D.

My brother, Joe Bader, a historian and union organizer with 30 years' experience, was one of my biggest supporters and best readers.

Well-known writer and editor Judith Levine, reviewed, corrected, and edited this book with a level of sophistication and expertise that, frankly, I had never before seen or experienced.

And, finally, my wife, Margot Duxler, has not only, as usual, been an indispensable reader and supportive critic of my writing, but has been my champion, partner, and lifeline throughout the process of writing and publishing this book. I can't possibly overestimate her foundational importance in my work and my life.

CPSIA information can be obtained
at www.ICGtesting.com
Printed in the USA
LVOW13s1450120617
537811LV00018B/108/P